Reinventing Co

From the Glob

C000153293

Reinventing Collective Action

From the Global to the Local

Edited by
Colin Crouch and David Marquand

Blackwell Publishers

Copyright © The Political Quarterly Publishing Co. Ltd.

ISBN 0–631–19721–4

First published 1995

Blackwell Publishers
108 Cowley Road, Oxford, OX4 1JF, UK.

and
238 Main Street,
Cambridge, MA. 02142, USA.

All rights reserved. Except for the quotation of short passages for the purposes of criticism and review, no part of this publication may be reproduced, stored in a retrieval system, or transmitted, in any form or by any means, electronic, mechanical, photocopying, recording or otherwise, without the prior permission of the publisher.

Except in the United States of America, this book is sold subject to the condition that it shall not, by way of trade or otherwise, be lent, resold, hired out, or otherwise circulated without the publisher's prior consent in any form of binding or cover other than that in which it is published and without a similar condition including this condition being imposed on the subsequent purchaser.

British Library Cataloguing in Publication Data
A catalogue record for this book is available from the British Library

Library of Congress Cataloging in Publication Data
Cataloging in Publication data applied for.

Typset by Joshua Associates Ltd., Oxford
Printed in Great Britain by Whitstable Litho, Kent.

CONTENTS

© The Political Quarterly Publishing Co. Ltd. 1995. Published by Blackwell Publishers, 108 Cowley Road, Oxford OX4 1JF, UK and 238 Main Street, Cambridge, MA 02142, USA.

PREFACE

THE OBJECT of this book is to further debate on the emerging new agenda of the left and centre-left—not just in Britain, but on the European continent and in North America as well. It was conceived at a conference at the University of Sheffield, organised jointly by the Political Economy Research Centre and THE POLITICAL QUARTERLY. In addition to the editors and authors of this book, participants at the conference include Tim Bale, Joanne Cook, Audrey Coppard, James Cornford, Bernard Crick, Joan Crouch, Malcolm Dean, Frank Field, Andrew Gamble, Randall Germain, A. H. Halsey, Mike Harris, Deborah Haythorne, Paul Hirst, Gavin Kelly, Judith Marquand, Sylvia McColm, Matthew Owen, Anthony Payne, Giles Radice, Sue Regan, Maurice Roche, Trevor Smith and Tony Wright. We are indebted to all of them for their insights and debating skills. We also wish to thank the Joseph Rowntree Reform Trust for financial support; Sylvia McColm for her tireless enthusiasm and efficiency as conference organiser; Audrey Coppard for her skilful and sensitive copy-editing; and Deborah Haythorne and the PERC and Politics Department graduate students, Tim Bale, Joanne Cook, Mike Harris and Gavin Kelly, for the time and energy they spent on making the conference a success.

Colin Crouch
David Marquand
The Editors
The Political Quarterly

© The Political Quarterly Publishing Co. Ltd. 1995. Published by Blackwell Publishers, 108 Cowley Road, Oxford OX4 1JF, UK and 238 Main Street, Cambridge, MA 02142, USA.

FOREWORD

GORDON BROWN*

A DISTINGUISHING feature of democratic socialism, both in Britain and around the world, has always been a belief in using the power of all of us to advance the good of each—collective action to help every individual to realise his or her potential. Indeed, socialists believe that human emancipation is impossible without action by the community to tackle the entrenched interests that hold individuals back and to provide people with the opportunity to realise their potential.

One hundred years ago, these guiding principles made action against poverty, slums and unemployment the priority of the Left, since people could not begin to realise their potential as long as they were denied adequate nourishment, proper housing and work. And fifty years ago, the post-war settlement, based on setting a floor of rights to social security, employment, healthcare and educational opportunities, was motivated by similar beliefs.

During the course of the post-war era, however, these collectivist principles began to fall into disrepute. Too often, collective solutions had slipped from being the means to the end of individual emancipation to appearing to be an end in themselves. By the end of the 1970s, the New Right had succeeded in painting collectivism not as a byword for emancipation, but for stifling, centralised state control. It was on this basis that they made the case for deregulation and the unrestrained free market as the route to individual empowerment.

Today, after a decade and a half of governing Britain, it is clear that the New Right has been unable to deliver on its emancipatory promises. Indeed, there is a growing recognition that the neo-liberal experiment has, once again, exposed the need for collective action as a route to individual emancipation. Old problems like structural unemployment, inadequate public services and insecurity at work, as well as new ones such as destabilising currency speculation and environmental degradation, make a compelling case for the relevance of collective action in the 1990s.

What is clear, however, is that the purposes and methods of collective solutions will be very different from those envisaged one hundred, fifty or even twenty years ago. First, it must be recognised that people no longer simply want protection by the state against barriers to emancipation. They need to be empowered by the community to use their own talents and exercise their own initiative. Secondly, collective action must not be automatically interpreted to mean intervention by the state, and must embrace other institutions.

* Gordon Brown, M.P., Shadow Chancellor of the Exchequer.

FOREWORD

As the historical analysis shows, the success of traditional collective solutions was, in general, limited to basic aims of fighting poverty and want. The tragedy today is that even in many industrialised countries, these social problems have reappeared. Looking around Europe and America today, therefore, it is clear that action by the community is essential to wage a new war on deprivation and underprivilege.

But, collective action in the 1990s and beyond must be about more than this. It must focus also on the politics of potential—taking radical measures to enable people to use their own talents to bridge the gap between what they are and what they have it in themselves to become. The emancipation of the individual, to paraphrase an old quotation, comes not from what the state can do for you but from what the state can enable you to do for yourself.

So, the welfare state must not simply be a safety net, but must offer new pathways out of poverty for people trapped on benefit. The education system must not simply be about a basic standard provided for people before they enter work, it must provide the opportunity for lifelong learning, so that everyone can acquire the skills they need to use their potential to the full. There must be a commitment to tackling the entrenched interests and accumulations of power and privilege that hold people back, and there must be a new constitutional settlement which allows people to take more control over their own lives.

Just as the ends of community action must be more ambitious and liberating, the means through which it is undertaken must also change to take account of new circumstances. It used to be thought by some on the Left that for the individual to have some control over the productive process in the public interest, the only possible mechanism was expropriation of the means of production and the abolition of markets. It is now clear that these conclusions do not follow, and that the key question is not whether we abolish markets, but how markets work in the public interest, and how we set standards to achieve this.

Too often for the Left, collective action has meant only state action by the nation state. Today, it is clear that the community must work not just through central government, but also through local government, voluntary organisations as well as collective organisations, like trade unions. For instance, funding for childcare, essential to empower women to go out to work, can be provided through a partnership between local authorities, employers and individuals.

Furthermore, it is also clear that, in today's emerging global economy, the destinies of different countries are inextricably linked. To secure the economic growth, environmental care and social harmony which are necessary for individual emancipation, governments must work together at a European level and beyond.

The task of re-inventing collective action is about finding new ways of using the power of the community to help the individual, and it is about building popular support for community action. It requires new thinking

3

© The Political Quarterly Publishing Co. Ltd. 1995.

about the role of government, not so much as owner or employer, as traditionally conceived, but as partner, enabler, catalyst and co-ordinator. Though not everyone will share every sentiment expressed in these pages, this book makes an original and compelling contribution to thinking about these and other central issues, and is therefore to be greatly welcomed.

© The Political Quarterly Publishing Co. Ltd. 1995.

© The Political Quarterly Publishing Co. Ltd. 1995. Published by Blackwell Publishers, 108 Cowley Road, Oxford OX4 1JF, UK and 238 Main Street, Cambridge, MA 02142, USA.

RE-INVENTING COLLECTIVE ACTION

COLIN CROUCH AND DAVID MARQUAND*

AFTER nearly two decades of confusion, a reborn collectivism has begun to challenge the neo-liberal orthodoxy which has shaped British public policy since the 1970s. But this new collectivism differs radically from the state-centred collectivism developed, largely by and through the Labour Party, in the interwar and postwar years. It is pluralistic, diverse and internationalist. It looks outwards to the institutions of global economic governance and to the supranational institutions of the European Union, and downwards to localities and regions. It embraces the traditional liberal concern with constitutional checks and balances to guard against the abuse of state power, and the traditional Christian democratic concern with subsidiarity and power sharing. Above all, it seeks a vibrant civil society, with flourishing intermediate institutions, some public, some private and some mixed, standing between the state and the individual. The chapters that follow address different aspects of this theme. Here we try to explore the central strands that bring them together, so as to stake out the terms of a new collectivism appropriate to the needs of the next century.

The fallacy of individualism

We begin by examining the failings of the particular, highly eccentric vision of individualism espoused by the New Right. In some of its guises, individualism is a noble concept. John Stuart Mill and Thomas Paine were both individualists. Individualism of the sort they espoused and developed protects us against arbitrary power. It grants us the freedom to lead our lives as we choose. It gives us incentives to be creative and resourceful. It also gives us the stern but necessary message that we must try to solve our problems by ourselves, without leaning on others, whether the state or other individuals. Societies without strong elements of that sort of individualism lack drive and initiative and the scope for innovation. Indeed, the respect for individuality and emphasis on personal fulfilment which lay at the heart of Paine's republicanisn and Mill's liberalism are equally central to the new collectivism. New Right individualism, however, is a very different creature. It embodies and perpetuates two major lies. First, it misleadingly suggests that social problems can and should be treated as a series of individual problems, to be solved by people acting alone. Second, to adopt Orwell's famous phrase about equality, it makes some individuals more individual than others.

*Colin Crouch and David Marquand are editors of this book.

The first lie is well recognised. John Donne got to the heart of it in his famous lines:

No man is an island entire of it self
But each is part of a continent.

Three implications follow. The first has to do with what economists call externalities. Many things that I might want to do adversely affect others; every time I start my car I produce noise and pollution for those around me. This has always been true, but modern technology has enormously magnified the scale of the phenomenon, and the risks associated with it. The extensions in our powers as individuals that allow us, the populations of the late 20th century, to look down on earlier generations because they relied excessively on collective action hugely increase the collective harm that we all do.

In many cases, moreover, these collective harms can be prevented or repaired only by collective remedies. Many of the 19th century battles between collectivists and advocates of *laissez faire* were fought over the public health and safety problems produced when industry brought people together in factories full of powerful machines and polluting processes, in cities of unprecedented size. Today's environmental problems are no different in kind, but frighteningly bigger in scale. The environmental dangers discussed in Paul Ekins's chapter in this book are the direct successors of the problems that inspired the environmental struggles of the Victorian period. They show that one frequent claim of neo-liberal politics—the claim that, as societies become richer and their members can do more for themselves, they have less need for collective action—is not merely untrue, but the reverse of the truth.

More positively, there are constructive things that can be achieved only through co-operation, by transcending individualism. The more that the central guidelines of our political economy force us into dog-eats-dog competition, the less we can reap the benefits of such opportunities. Michael Piore draws attention to the benefits which businesses have reaped through co-operation, in societies where institutional mechanisms are in place to enable it to thrive. In Britain, where even hospitals and local general practitioners are now required to deal with each other at arm's length through analogues of market relationships, we have been moving in the opposite direction.

One familiar New-Right response to such arguments is to insist that if something is not provided by the market, no one can 'really' want it; and that, if no one really wants, those who say they want it must be paternalistic busy-bodies. There are many examples of that response in current public policy. The more sophisticated have a better answer. They will admit that certain collective needs require attention, but argue that state action to adjust market incentives can induce private firms to take the necessary steps. Thus, regulatory mechanisms can replace public ownership for natural monopolies; industrial processes that cause environmental

6

© The Political Quarterly Publishing Co. Ltd. 1995.

damage can be taxed instead of being prohibited; tax concessions can induce sufficient private sponsorship to render public support for the arts or sport unnecessary.

These arguments should be taken seriously. There are good grounds for exploring the scope for regulatory and other devices that will enable behaviour governed by a market model to help contribute to chosen collective goals. Here, there is room for dialogue between individualists and collectivists; and perhaps for the development of new consensus between them. But there is no reason to endorse an ideological preference for market solutions if their adoption would distort the policy goal. For example, it is foolish to reject public ownership in cases where it would serve the required ends more simply and directly than regulation. And sometimes, as with the internal market of the National Health Service and the use of league tables to assist parents in school choice, the search for surrogate market signals may distort the criteria on which decisions are based.

The second lie is more serious. When the New Right speaks of individuals, it does not always mean human individuals. Sometimes, of course, it does. When it insists that people should stand on their own feet and eschew state dependency; when workers are told they should not be represented by trade unions, but should become individual achievers within their companies; or when people are told that they should become self-employed and give up the benefit of employment rights or social insurance, New Right individualism really does refer to the vulnerable human person. But, in a deep irony, when the rhetoric of individualism is used to extol the entrepreneurs and political leaders who are held up to us as its epitome, it means something altogether different. Here 'individual' is used in the fundamentally deceptive sense of 'person able to mobilise the resources of a large, privately-owned collective unit'.

English common law and classical economics know only individuals; they find it hard to deal with collective entities. Both solve this problem by treating them as though they were individuals, most notably in giving companies the legal status of persons. Most of the time this is a harmless and useful convenience. But when it is used to obfuscate the distinction between fictional persons, such as ICI, and real ones, such as ICI's employees, the consequences are deeply damaging. The entrepreneurs and business leaders who are held to embody the virtues of individualism hardly ever act as individuals themselves. They are permanently surrounded by consultants, entourages, expensive professional advisers. The managers who tell their employees that they must act as, and be treated as, individuals instead of leaning on the collective crutch of a trade union, do not abide by their own precepts. Their firms surround them with a protective wall of staff; experts in management tell them how to mould the behaviour of the lonely, ill-informed crowd that constitutes their employees; if they experience strain in performing their tasks, the firms will even provide specialists in stress management to help them.

7

© The Political Quarterly Publishing Co. Ltd. 1995.

The truth is that the modern business firm is itself a collectivity. Firms bring together and co-ordinate resources on an extensive scale. The legal and political fiction that enables their actions to be classified as individual and not as collective does not inhibit their capacity to act as collectivities. Indeed, it is on that capacity that their competitive power in the market place depends. Farming out public functions to firms, on the grounds that individual initiative is to be preferred to collective action, does not lessen the quantum of collective action within society. It takes functions away from certain collectivities and transfers them to others. In doing so it privileges business authority over other entitlements to participate in collective decision making. It narrows the public realm, so that the rest of the population can participate in public affairs only through an occasional vote. By the same token, attempts to deny other organised interests political influence, on the grounds that democracy means the representation of individuals and not of groups, do not promote a polity in which individuals are the only actors. Insofar as they are successful (and it is important to emphasise that they have not been completely successful either in Britain or elsewhere) they produce a polity in which only those people who control organisations that are artificially treated as individuals, in other words business firms, can organise effective lobbies or provide the personnel to man public bodies.

As well as deflecting our attention from necessary collective tasks, in short, New Right individualism is a mechanism for giving political influence to certain sorts of people, and for denying it to others—in practice, for restricting it to those who can wield the resources of business firms. When we are told that we are self-reliant individuals, strong enough to do without the old props of collectivities, the message may seem flattering. What it really means, however, is that we are politically alone: alone in a world where vast resources are mobilised by tight collectivities of wealth-controllers and managers. And because we are alone, we are de-politicised.

Capitalism unchained

The changing fortunes of the collectivist and individualist strands in Britain's political economy, and the impact on them of the neo-liberal renaissance of the 1970s and 1980s, fall into place against this background. As contemporaries were well aware, the late 19th century saw a marked shift away from the individualism of earlier decades towards a greater emphasis on collective action. State regulation was introduced in policy area after policy area, to protect society from such externalities as health-damaging pollution, industrial accidents and the adulteration of consumer products. Trade-union action in restraint of trade—anathema to the common law—was slowly legalised. Social reformers began to advocate positive action, either by public authorities or by private

8

charities, to alleviate poverty. Municipalities like Joe Chamberlain's Birmingham began to lay the foundations for what was sometimes known as 'gas and water socialism'. Between the wars, the economic collectivism of the rising Labour Party came increasingly to the fore. Collectivists came to believe that competitive capitalism was economically inefficient, especially in the provision of basic needs. State planning and state owner-ship were advocated partly as ways to dispossess capitalists and redistri-bute wealth, and partly to make the economy more productive. A few also advocated them on the grounds that they would enable workers to participate in—or, in more radical formulations to control—the govern-ment of industry.

Only parts of this agenda were entrenched in the settlement hammered out under the wartime coalition and the post-war Labour Government. Some allegedly 'basic' industries were nationalised, but financial services—the true commanding heights of any capitalist economy—were left untouched. Largely because the trade unions were at best ambivalent about workers' control, and at worst downright hostile to it, no significant moves were made towards industrial co-determination of the sort that grew up in Federal Germany during the same period. Vigorous and unsleeping trade-union hostility to any form of state intervention in the labour market, except in the shortest of short terms as a mechanism of crisis management, also rendered the Government's early planning ambitions nugatory. In practice, planning was redefined to mean Keynesian demand management—in essence a form of liberal collectiv-ism, designed to make it possible to combine the collectivist goal of full employment with market allocation of resources in a new synthesis. It was in the welfare state, not particularly valued by the socialist pioneers, that collective provision was most firmly embedded; and, like Keynesian full employment, the welfare state was underpinned by a broad national con-sensus, extending right across the political spectrum.

The roots of this consensus went deep. Its intellectual progenitors included social imperialists and social liberals as well as democratic socialists; among the social interests that helped to construct it, the profes-sional service class was as prominent as the labour movement. That said, it is important to recognise that the reformed welfare capitalism of the post-war period was also the product of a conscious decision on the part of western governments to seek an alternative to the economic stagnation and social instability which had paved the way for fascism between the wars; and to find an answer to the internal and external threat of Soviet communism after 1945. In the early post-war years, capitalism was on the defensive, morally and politically, all over western Europe. It recovered quite quickly; but the capitalism that recovered was the capitalism of the New Deal and the Marshall Plan, of Keynes, Jean Monnet and the architects of the German social-market economy, not the capitalism of Herbert Hoover. And one of the reasons why business elites made their peace with the Keynesian welfare state as quickly and as easily as they did

9

is that they correctly believed themselves to be engaged in world-wide competition with the Soviet model.

Now the wheel has come full circle. The inflationary crises of the 1970s, the political victories of the right during the 1980s, and, above all, profound changes in the global political economy have created a new configuration, closer, in some ways, to that of the late-nineteenth century than to that of the long boom of the post-war period. Intensified international competition, the changes in productive processes made possible by information technology, a sharp decline in the returns to unskilled labour, the destruction of old barriers of habit and prejudice that kept women out of the labour force and the globalisation of capital markets have, between them, destroyed the male-dominated, mass-production-based, full-employment system of the post-war period. Many employers have reacted by insisting that they can remain competitive only by cutting labour costs, by worsening working conditions, by casualising employment and (in North America more than in Europe) by lowering real wages. Meanwhile, the internal and external challenges to western capitalism represented by powerful Communist parties on the one hand, and an apparently strong and expansionist Soviet bloc on the other, have disappeared. The working class, at least in the sense of groups of employees with an alternative political identity and organisations capable of pressing their interests, has shrunk drastically; and the political parties that used to represent it have become correspondingly weaker.

The results are familiar. The balance of economic power between capital and labour has shifted in favour of the former; and the balance of political power has followed suit. Markets have been deregulated to face competition, enabling capital to move around the world in search of labour; and unskilled labour, at any rate, is in over-supply. As the need to attract capital to invest in national currencies looms larger than the need to maintain employment, control of inflation acquires a higher priority and full employment a lower one. The collapse of the old Keynesian priorities imparts a deflationary bias to economic policy. The corresponding shift in the balance of political power produces a bias in favour of high earners and a policy shift towards low taxation. That shift has been reinforced by the erosion of political loyalties engendered by social and cultural change. Parties need to attract voters more energetically than they used to do; and, by a cruel irony, they discover that, when incomes are increasingly insecure, one of the easiest ways to do this is to promise reductions in taxation. Even if the main beneficiaries are high earners, such promises can be universally popular. To the extent that they are, electoral competition increasingly takes the form of a tax-cutting auction. This, in turn, threatens the welfare state and intensifies the insecurities which made tax cuts attractive in the first place.

There is a further irony as well. Through all these crises, businesses have been able to produce an ever-growing array of goods and services at lower cost. Management skills have similarly advanced. For ordinary people the

10

upshot is growing insecurity at work, in the welfare state and in public space more generally. One area of life, however, continues to hold out promise: goods in the shops that can make private life brighter. The lower our taxes, the less generous our welfare state, the longer our working hours and the cheaper the goods we import from abroad, the more of these we can buy. The individualism of the private citizen becomes ever more private, but, as corporations take over the functions relinquished by a hollowed-out state, the individualism of those who control the corporate world becomes ever more powerful, politically as well as economically. The grim lives of the late 19th century working class produced an orientation to the collectivity that generated the political movements which eventually gave birth to the welfare state and mixed economy. At first sight, the consumer lives of the heterogeneous populations of the late 20th century seem more likely to lock those who live them into a self-reinforcing spiral of depoliticisation and individualisation.

The contradictions of neo-liberalism

Yet there are increasing signs that the neo-liberal system is not as hermetically sealed as this implies. Two sets of chinks have appeared in its armour. First, the deterioration of the collective spaces which an individualistic world neglects bears ever harder on individuals. There is uneasiness over environmental damage; there is frustration over the myriad problems which a dogmatic preference for individual as against collective solutions produces in such fields as transport and urban development; most obviously there is growing concern over crime.

There are deeper internal contradictions in the neo-liberal model as well. Unchained capitalism depends simultaneously on driving down work security and on encouraging consumer expenditure. But much of the latter depends on consumer confidence—particularly, on the belief by consumers that they can afford major purchases. This is particularly important in the case of house purchase—until recently the chief mechanism for encouraging middle-income people to identify with property-owning individualism—but similar arguments apply to all forms of consumer credit. The wealthy invite the rest of us to copy their consumption patterns, and expect us to share their political perspectives when we have done so. But the changing distribution of income (especially post-tax income) reduces our abilities to do this. People are unlikely to take big risks as consumers when they are told that they must expect their jobs to be temporary and their weekly earnings unpredictable, especially if the prop of welfare state security is withdrawn at the same time. It might be possible to persuade a salaried work force, with secure pension provisions, to view the welfare state as an instrument of paternalistic collectivism, and to conclude that strong individuals should buy insurance, health and education in the market place. But as competitive pressures intensify,

11

© The Political Quarterly Publishing Co. Ltd. 1995.

and labour casualisation spreads from the unskilled to the skilled, and from the skilled to management itself, the insecure become ever-more numerous. For these reasons the triumph of New Right individualism has been Pyrrhic; or, in the less elevated language of current debate, economic recovery seems to have brought a 'feel-bad' instead of a 'feel-good' factor.

Less obvious contradictions are to be found on the global level. The wild oscillations of the currency markets which are the concomitants of de-regulation make it possible for foreign exchange dealers to make huge profits, but they represent a heavy cost to productive industry, above all to exporters. Indeed, one of the main arguments for a monetary union in the core of the European Union is that the cost of hedging against currency fluctuations is a serious burden on the manufacturing sector and therefore depresses industrial investment. The export-oriented capitalisms of East Asia depend on selling their goods in western markets, but the deflationary bias fostered by intensifying global competition makes it more difficult for them to do this; and that, in turn, makes global competition more cut-throat. Environmental degradation in the Third World endangers the entire planet; social dislocation in the former Soviet Union raises the spectre of an authoritarian backlash; both are exacerbated by the neo-liberal orthodoxies which the IMF and World Bank impose on weak economies.

Beyond the Nation State

There is, therefore, ample scope for redefined collectivist solutions. But the redefinition must be radical. For most of the post-war period, as we have seen, the term 'collective action' was treated as a virtual synonym for 'state action'. The post-war Labour Government turned its back on the 'gas and water socialism' of the pioneers and took it for granted, both in the economic and in the social domains, that nationalisation was *ipso facto* preferable to municipalisation. Gas, electricity and the hospital service—all of which had strong municipal components before 1945—were all nationalised. The Labour Government of the 1960s took the process a stage further when it forced unwilling local authorities to introduce comprehensive schools. By the same token, the Attlee Government refused to take part in what became the European Coal and Steel Community, on the grounds that supranational institutions would undermine the sovereignty of the central state, and majority sentiment in the Labour movement continued to view the process of European integration askance until well into the 1980s.

Behind all this lay the tacit assumption that the road to collective provision lay, and could only lie, through victory in a general election, leading to control of the absolutely sovereign Westminster Parliament. Local government was somehow inferior to national government; supranational integration was a threat to it. That was the apparent moral of Labour's

12

victory in the 1945 election; it was reinforced in 1966. As James K. Galbraith's chapter shows, it is profoundly dangerous today. In a world of global companies, global capital markets and global communications, in which the pressures of global competition are the chief enemies of community values and collectivitist practice, an exclusive focus on the nation-state makes sense only for the New Right. It may be argued that it was the actions of nation-states—and still more their failures to act—which let the genie of unchained global capitalism out of the bottle, rather than technological or cultural change. But even if this is true, it does not follow that nation-states can put the genie back. That can be done only by international and supranational institutions, created by nation-states acting together, but with competences and capacities which no single nation-state can match. To cling to national sovereignty in the world of the 1990s is, in practice, to hand sovereignty over to the global marketplace.

There is, in fact, a logic in the New Right's vehement opposition to transfers of authority and competence from the national level to the supranational institutions of the European Union. The prevailing view that Eurosceptics stand for national sovereignty, while pro-Europeans are happy to dilute it, is valid only on assumption that sovereignty is a purely legal and political matter, with no economic content. For the New Right, for which interference with market forces is, by definition, illegitimate, that assumption is both a political convenience and a logical imperative. In a world of intensifying international competition and growing economic interdependence, it is a perverse absurdity for everyone else. Which represents the greater threat to national self-determination—a treaty requirement to accept qualified majority decisions even if it means being on the losing side, or a requirement to abandon chosen social and fiscal policies in the face of undercutting in world markets?

Much the same applies, though in a more complex way, to the internal governance of the nation-state, and to the relationship between the state and civil society. Here too there is a logic in the New Right's approach. It is a commonplace that, in the 1980s and early 1990s, central government has steadily eroded the powers of local government. At first sight, this creeping centralism might seem inconsistent with the pluralism that neo-liberal individualism would appear to imply. They can, however, be reconciled. For the New Right, one of the virtues of a market system is indeed its centrifugal character. Power is fragmented and pushed out to a mass of different points in society; we do not have to worry whether rulers are good or wise, because we do not depend on them for much. If everyone is subject to market competition, no-one has authority, and the state is reduced to a minimal role. To achieve this dominance of the market system, however, power must constantly be exercised against those who wish to challenge it, to dilute it or to impede it. Such political power as remains in a marketised society has to be gathered into the hands of a tightly controlled centre to which only those favourable to the market systems can gain access.

13

© The Political Quarterly Publishing Co. Ltd. 1995.

COLIN CROUCH AND DAVID MARQUAND

By the same token, the left and centre-left have rightly become more reserved about the central state than they used to be, and correspondingly more anxious to disperse political power. Three reasons stand out. The first is that, by a quirk of history, parties based on the old working class are now in the position faced by Christian democracy after the Second World War. In a secularising and urbanising society Christian Democrats feared their constituencies would shrink and their chances of winning majorities would be small. Their support for pluralism and subsidiarity was instrumental as well as ideological in character. Pluralism offered the prospect of a politics of coalition-building, in which they might have at least some influence on decisions without winning a majority; subsidiarity offered a path to power on the local or regional level, where national minorities might, in some cases, form majorities. The parallel with the socialist and social-democratic parties of today is self-evident.

Secondly, local and regional economic development, of the sort Michael Piore describes, increasingly offers a more fruitful focus for collective action than planning or regulation by the central state. It is a commonplace that the instruments with which post-war nation-states intervened in their economies have little purchase on the fluid, rapidly changing, interdependent economies of today. That is one of the reasons for the New Right's victory over old style, central-state collectivism. But this does not mean that public power has no role to play in economic life. What it means is that public power has to be deployed in much more subtle ways, and on different levels of government. On the local and regional levels, partnerships between the public and private sectors can and do contribute impressively to the pursuit of competitive advantage in the global marketplace. This is true even in Britain, where the reigning orthodoxy views such partnerships askance. Even under the Thatcher and Major governments, public-private partnerships have unobtrusively helped to foster economic development and regeneration in a number of city-regions, while appointed bodies like TECs and Development Corporations have sometimes become focal points for defining and articulating local interests. Experience in other European countries, as well as in the United States, suggests that more autonomous local governments could forge much more effective partnerships of this sort.

Thirdly, and most importantly, the values of the new collectivism are inherently pluralistic. The object of collective action is, after all, to empower individuals, to foster autonomy, to facilitate personal growth and self-realisation. For neo-liberals, empowerment and autonomy come only through market relationships, through free exchanges between atomistic individuals, pursuing their own self-interest as they see it. The political realm, and the negotiation and debate which are inseparable from it, are suspect. Exit is the only guarantee of freedom; voice carries the threat of coercion. The new collectivism accepts that markets can indeed empower; that today's consumers, ranging the shelves of Safeway or sunning themselves on Mediterranean beaches, enjoy important freedoms

14

© The Political Quarterly Publishing Co. Ltd. 1995.

which were not available to their grandparents. But it does not accept that markets are the only means of empowerment, or even the most important ones. It seeks empowerment through voice as well as through exit; through the debate and negotiation of the 'democratic, civic community' discussed in William Sullivan's chapter in this book, as well as through the free exchanges of the market-place. But if the much-abused term 'community' is to have meaning, it must be embodied in the lives and actions of real people, in real places, assuming responsibility for their own affairs. Communities are, by definition, diverse. Empowerment through community must come from the bottom up.

Agenda for Institution-Building

All this implies a formidable institutional agenda, on every level of government. This is most obviously true of the global level discussed by James K. Galbraith. It is a truism that the world needs a new Bretton Woods—that the golden age of tamed, relatively stable, welfare capitalism which came to an end in the 1970s was a product of global order deliberately created, in the teeth of enormous difficulties, by the post-war generation; and that the ecological and social devastation which are the hallmarks of the current disorder cannot be addressed unless and until a new global order is brought into being. It is equally plain that the existing institutions of global economic governance are not up to the job.

Yet the reasons for their inadequacy need a more tough-minded analysis than the conventional wisdom of the centre-left can supply. *Bien pensant* liberals and socialists often forget that the Bretton Woods system was part and parcel of a wider *pax Americana*, dependent on American economic and military power. As in the days of the nineteenth-century *pax Britannica*, the global order was kept orderly by a hegemonic global policeman, rich and strong enough to assume the responsibilities involved. Now there is no hegemon; and it can safely be prophesied that we shall not see another in the foreseeable future.

This does not mean that there is no point in trying to work for a new Bretton Woods, and for reformed global institutions with the capacity and will to cope with the consequences of the untamed, unstable, increasingly non-welfare capitalism of our time. As James K. Galbraith and Paul Ekins both show, in different ways, such institutions are desperately needed. What it does mean is that success is unlikely to come quickly—partly because of the familiar problem of the free rider which always bedevils attempts to promote the general good through negotiations between sovereign nations acting in a Hobbesian state of nature, and partly because too many such nations are still dazzled by New Right theology. To mention only the most obvious example, the America of Newt Gingrich does not bear much resemblance to the America of Franklin Roosevelt

15

© The Political Quarterly Publishing Co. Ltd. 1995.

and Harry Truman. For a long time to come, waiting for collectivist enlightenment to dawn in Washington will be like waiting for Godot.

A British government anxious to reinvent collective action would work for radical reform of the IMF and World Bank so as to correct their deflationary biases and make them more responsive both to the demands of environmental sustainability and to the needs of the Third World and the post-Communist societies of Eastern Europe and the former Soviet Union. It would also work for international agreement to stabilise exchange rates and, in Will Hutton's phrase, to bring the world's financial markets to heel.[1] But it would be unwise to put all its eggs in the basket of international negotiation. It is on the European, not the global, level that Britain can work most effectively for a more orderly world economy, and with and through the European Union that the pressures of unchained capitalism and the threat of increasing environmental degradation can best be countered. In the absence of a global policeman, regionalisation—the gradual emergence of multi-national regional blocks—provides the most promising path to a sane world order. Regional blocks also provide the safest available havens from the current disorder.

Of these blocks, the European Union is the oldest, the most developed and the best equipped for collective action. It also has the most to lose if it fails to act with the speed and on the scale that the times require. European welfare capitalism, the great, historic achievement of the post-war years and one of the greatest achievements of European civilisation, is now in jeopardy. It cannot be saved by the individual Member States of the Union acting separately. Their only hope of exerting pressure on a world economy which is spinning out of control—and of protecting themselves from accelerating social degradation if it remains out of control—is to act together, through the institutions of the Union itself.

However weak those institutions may be, they do at least exist. They also have a proven capacity for rapid growth in times of crisis. More important still, the Union can draw on political traditions—social democracy, Christian Democracy, even French Gaullism in some of its guises—instinctively hostile to unchained capitalism and sceptical of the free-market shibboleths which have helped to engender it. European publics still cling to the values and practices of social citizenship which the pressures of the global market-place are now threatening to overwhelm; the Union's institutions still embody them. This, of course, is why New Right Britain has deliberately distanced itself from mainland Europe and set its face against further transfers of sovereignty to Brussels, Luxembourg and Strasbourg.

For the same reason, however, a Labour or Lib-Lab Britain would be close to the European mainstream. Such a Britain would need to be part of a strong, well-integrated Union, willing and able to deploy its considerable bargaining power in the interests of exchange-rate stability and sustain-

[1] Will Hutton, *The State We're In*, Jonathan Cape, London, 1995, p. 313.

© The Political Quarterly Publishing Co. Ltd. 1995.

able growth and prepared, if necessary, to sacrifice free-trade orthodoxy for the sake of social justice and cohesion. As John Pinder argues, the re-invention of collective action on the European level also implies further positive integration, balancing the negative integration of the single market. All this entails radical institutional reform. For the reasons Pinder gives, it must, in the first place, entail a more powerful European Parliament, with legislative teeth as strong as those of the Council of Ministers, acting as a constant source of pressure to realise the ideal of social citizenship on the European as well as on the national level. It also entails swifter decision-making, and therefore more majority voting, in the Council of Ministers, as well as a more powerful Commission, firmly rooted in the democratically-elected Parliament.

But that is only part of the moral of the last decade and a half. The familiar, small 'l' liberal case for decentralised government and constitutional checks and balances—that an over-centralised and over-mighty state may threaten individual freedom and civil rights—has been hugely reinforced by the experience of the Thatcher and Major years. But, as we tried to show above, there is a collectivist case as well as a liberal one; and that too has acquired new force and urgency of late. A precondition of effective collective action in this country is to apply the Christian Democratic principle of subsidiarity, which New Right British ministers misuse to justify their foot-dragging over positive integration in the European union, to the internal governance of Britain. And that principle logically entails checks and balances.

The democratic deficit

A less obvious implication follows as well. Part of the point of reinventing collective action is to make irresponsible power accountable, to give ordinary men and women a say in the decisions that shape their lives. Who is to guard the guardians? How do we ensure that collective institutions are themselves accountable to the collectivities in whose names they act? The New Right's answer is to marketise them. Not surprisingly, that has turned out to be no answer. But the question remains; and if the Left is to win the battle of ideas instead of relying on an evanescent victory in the battle for votes, it will have to find an answer. In particular, it will have to find an answer to the yawning democratic deficit which is to be found, not only on the European level, where the term was first coined, but on every level of government.

On the European level, there is not much doubt about what needs to be done. The problem lies in the doing. Westminster politicians who oppose moves towards a federal Europe on the grounds that it would weaken parliamentary democracy have grasped the wrong end of the stick. For democrats, at least, the problem with the European Union is not that it is too federal, but that it is not federal enough. In a wide range of policy areas,

17

© The Political Quarterly Publishing Co. Ltd. 1995.

as John Pinder points out, decisions are already taken by European institutions, not by national ones; and in these areas Westminster sovereignty is a fiction. The trouble is that, in the clumsy, opaque, proto-federal system we now have, too much power lies with the interlocking technocracies of the Council, the Commission and the great, private-sector corporations with an effective lobbying presence in Brussels, and too little with elected politicians. In a proper federation, with a clear separation of powers between different tiers of government, decision making would be far more transparent and therefore far more accountable than it is now. Progress will be slow, but there is no doubt that that is the direction in which a reforming British government should try to move.

The governance of Britain presents much greater problems. As Anthony Lester shows, the constitution is a seamless web. With the possible exception of proportional representation (which would not be regarded as a constitutional question in most democracies), reform in one sphere is bound to have consequences for others. A democratic legislature must have an elected second chamber. But what constituencies should it represent, and in what way? A bill of rights, enabling the courts to strike down legislation that infringes it, raises the question of judicial reform. Home Rule for Scotland and Wales raises the question of England's place in what would be at least a quasi-federal system. The decentralisation of government in England raises the question of how the new arrangements are to be entrenched. Because of all this, piecemeal ad hocery, the favourite standby of the British political class since the Glorious Revolution, is a recipe for muddle, self-contradiction and failure. As Lester argues, what appears at first sight to be a revolutionary alternative—a Constitutional Convention, followed by a Referendum—is in fact a far more realistic vehicle for change than a series of ordinary bills. It is, of course, a break with precedent. But there is no precedent for turning Britain's *ancien regime* into a democracy.

Towards a new Social Coalition

The crucial problem of agency remains. At the moment of writing, the Labour Party has an unprecedented lead in the opinion polls. It may still have one when this book is published. Conceivably, the next election will see a Conservative debacle on the scale of 1906 or 1945. But, to put it at its lowest, no one should count on it. In any case, collective action of the sort, and on the scale, envisaged in this book cannot be reinvented simply by winning a parliamentary election, no matter how crushing the majority.

If the changes advocated here are to be woven into the social fabric—and there is little point in making them if they are not—they will have to be supported by a new social coalition that endures through bad times as well as good. The elements of such a coalition lie all around us. As the jugger-naut of free-market individualism rolls on, losers begin to outnumber

18

winners. But, almost by definition, this potential coalition is extraordinarily diverse; also by definition, it extends well beyond Labour's core constituency. Parts of it have no feeling for the culture and traditions of the Labour movement. Other parts regard the tiniest deviation from that culture as a symptom of treachery. There is no reason of principle why it cannot be welded together. The fashionable post-modernist view that we live in a post-political age, in which political leadership is redundant and political mobilisation impossible, smacks of a teleology as dangerous as Sidney Webb's inevitability of gradualness or Karl Marx's dialectical materialism. But there is no denying that doing so will test the skill and courage of the Labour leadership to the utmost.

On a deeper and more important level, we speak of a social coalition, not just of a political one. A vision of collective action that embraces more than the central state cannot be realised solely, or even mainly, through the familiar mechanisms of party politics. It must be embodied in a variety of institutions and practices—local authorities, churches, charities, community groups, business associations—that transcend the logic of untrammelled individualism. The new collectivism cannot be the property of any one political party or movement. It will flourish only in so far as it enters the bloodstream of the wider society.

© The Political Quarterly Publishing Co. Ltd. 1995.

© The Political Quarterly Publishing Co. Ltd. 1995. Published by Blackwell Publishers, 108 Cowley Road, Oxford OX4 1JF, UK and 238 Main Street, Cambridge, MA 02142, USA.

RE-INVENTING COMMUNITY: PROSPECTS FOR POLITICS

WILLIAM M. SULLIVAN*

Democracy and Community

THIS is a perplexing moment at which to consider the relationship between community and politics. Certain kinds of politically-charged community appear to be flourishing. Nationalist movements of various stripes sow vigour in many places, often within and against existing national states. These movements are sometimes assisted and sometimes rivalled by newly-ascendant political tendencies which mobilise communities of identity around religious conviction. At the same time, the citizens of the leading industrial nations seem to be more divided and sceptical of the possibilities for democratic collective action than at any time since the Second World War. They feel less and less connected to each other and their governments, and at the very moment when the restructuring of the global economic and political order is forcing crucial choices upon all societies.

The difficulty of the moment was poignantly illustrated by a poll taken by *The New York Times* to commemorate the twenty-fifth anniversary of the Apollo Space Programme's successful moon expedition. The poll discovered that Americans now look back to the summer of 1969, even recognising its racial and political divisions, as a lost moment of national togetherness through identification with a great collective enterprise. Watching the Moon Walk of Neil Armstrong had provided a sense of national community, however transitory, which the respondents doubted could be achieved today.

While allowing for the inevitable softening effects of nostalgia, this finding remains disturbing. At the least it seems to record a weakening of confidence in collective political capacity to respond and to act. But it is also worth noting that the Apollo expedition of 1969 gave us the striking photographic image of 'Earth Rise', that most arresting icon of the environmental movement. It was the first time human beings had ever viewed their planet from the outside. 'Earth Rise' was a visual, visceral awakening to the common human dependence upon the well-being of the earth. At the same time, it dramatically underscored the fact of global interdependence, with the clear implication that mutual cooperation and

* William M. Sullivan is Professor of Philosophy at La Salle University in Philadelphia. Sullivan received his PhD in Philosophy from Fordham University. He writes on social and political philosophy, ethics, and philosophy of the social sciences. He is co-author of *Habits of the Heart* and *The Good Society*, author of *Reconstructing Public Philosophy*, and most recently, *Work and Integrity: The Crisis and Promise of Professionalism in American Life.*

20

responsibility are no longer impractical ideals, if they ever were only that, but have become the basic imperatives for survival.

The moon expedition took place near the end of the long period of postwar prosperity in the industrialised nations, just at the beginning of the unravelling of that international political economic order which had allowed a considerable measure of national social and economic community. That order had been established and guided by the United States, in part for geopolitical reasons; but it was in Western Europe, including Britain, that the possibilities of social democratic corporatism and the welfare state were most fully realised.

There the Keynesian management of national economies, including the public cooperation of oligopolistic business with labour and government, produced a dynamic yet stable record of economic growth plus significant improvement in socio-economic equity and welfare. Predictable political and economic environments promoted not only growth in employment and income, but some sense of moral vision and national community. In retrospect, that postwar order represented a remarkable, if flawed and fragile, political achievement. Distance, and the far harsher climate of the present, have tended to wrap it, too, in nostalgic mists. This is perhaps particularly so for the Left.

Our present condition seems to be a painfully contradictory one, in some ways the near-antithesis of the postwar heyday of international economic stability and national welfare corporatism. The end of the Cold War and the increasing movement toward a European economic union have opened new possibilities for cooperation which the polarised politics of the superpower era foreclosed. At the same time, dizzying techno-logical advance together with the internationalising of capital have dramatically increased the degree and complexity of interdependence within and among national societies. yet this interdependence is develop-ing largely without intention or plan, growing over the heads of the participants, benefiting and strengthening some while impoverishing and excluding others, and therefore spreading incomprehension and fear nearly everywhere.

The disarray currently visible throughout the polities of the developed nations, not least in the United States as well as the European Community, stands out in high relief against the very different picture which obtained through the postwar decades. We stand, that is, at the end of the utility of the social democratic, corporatist model of politics which empowered national governments to act for the benefit of the whole society. Granted that the degree of social solidarity and extent of inclusiveness varied greatly among the Atlantic nations, in retrospect, it is clear that from 1945 through at least the 1960s a roughly common set of institutional policies and understandings shaped the relations between the economy and society.

National economies were regulated along Keynesian lines, while the United States, locked in conflict with its now defunct superpower rival,

21

© The Political Quarterly Publishing Co. Ltd. 1995.

played the role of stimulator and stabiliser of the international system. Regardless of the degree to which they embraced universal inclusion and equality in principle, electorates, political parties, and leaders found these goals credible, because they seemed at once plausible and in the evident self-interest of the electoral majority. Buoyed by the long postwar boom, these were the policies of 'economic growth' and 'social welfare' which were administered by greatly expanded ranks of public administrators who acted above or beside a less ideologically-charged electoral politics. Throughout this period, important aspects of the American conception of the world order defined the horizon of politics, especially commitment to promoting economic 'growth' by private market actors as a superordinate and self-evident good.

Today's reality is quite disturbingly different. The source of the disturbance is the realisation that the era of internationalised capital, styled the global economy, is proving to be a time of social polarisation. The pursuit of economic growth by private market actors no longer produces automatic improvements in the standard of living for the majority of the electorate in any given national society. Some individuals, firms, industries, and regions become winners in a wildly volatile though intensely competitive situation, while others lose, dramatically and sometimes catastrophically. Because the key actors such as multinational finance and corporations are increasingly transnational in scale, national states find themselves less and less able to control their economic destiny—any more than they can readily control their cultural, linguistic, or demographic destinies.

The political consequence of this sudden decline in the capacity of states to protect their societies has been fragmentation and disillusionment. The social consequence, which both fuels the political effects and is exacerbated by them, is the generation of an elite of winners in the new economy which is less integrated with the national society and consequently increasingly irresponsible toward it. These cosmopolitan individualists with few local loyalties, while often prominent and sometimes powerful, are relatively few.

This secession of the successful is grimly complemented by the increasing number of newly marginalised persons and groups, once economically secure or expectant, who now find themselves facing highly uncertain prospects. While they, too, for different reasons, now distrust the national state, they can find no standing in the trans-national networks which sustain the new elite. Not unnaturally, such citizens are often resentful and find themselves susceptible to the appeal of various forms of identity politics which promise solidarity and significance, sometimes on the basis of ethnic, racial, regional, religious, or other particularity.

This polarisation of advanced societies into cosmopolitan individualists who travel morally light, on the one hand, and the newly marginal and resentful on the other, does not bode well for the traditional goals of the Left. Yet the achievement of a high degree of democratic inclusion,

22

© The Political Quarterly Publishing Co. Ltd. 1995.

equality, dignity, and solidarity are evidently in the not-too-long-term interest of every society. Managing the capriciously fluid and brutally unequal state of global interdependence is a common necessity at this *fin-de-siecle*. In this important way, the tradition of the democratic Left has never been more important, nor more realistic.

The clear imperative is to find ways to turn the growing links of national and global connection to mutual advantage rather than allowing what seems an all too evident drift toward heightened polarisation between the successful and the marginal, a morally odious polarisation with dangerous implications at both the national and the transnational level. At the same time, there is the apparent unwillingness or inability of most political actors, including the most powerful, to organise their policies towards this end. At such a moment, how can advocates for the traditions of social democracy and democratic community take their bearings? More specifically, what role is there for the notion of democratic community, once a primary end of the politics of the Left, yet today a notion which seems to be receding in the popular imagination while it is being sacrificed to the putative demands of economic efficiency and political realism?

These are the issues explored, albeit with the limitations inherent in an American perspective, in what follows. More specifically, I wish to explore, and if possible defend, the thesis that achieving the democratic goals which the Left has championed today requires vigorous civic community as its key enabling condition. That is, the effort to uphold and sustain the ethos of solidarity, with its implication of equal dignity within an inclusive polity that aims to equalise life-chances for all citizens, will require a new emphasis upon the development of forms and understanding of politics which I will call democratic civic community.

I want to explore this thesis in two stages, by asking two questions. First, why has the growth society model remained so attractive, despite its obviously unsatisfactory political and social consequences, throughout the postwar era, but especially in the wake of the ending of the Cold War? Does its appeal perhaps lie as much (or more) in ideology than in results? That is, does the promise of opportunity conjoined to minimal demands for responsibility exercise an unrealistic hold on contemporary political understanding, despite such evident social 'externalities' as class polarisation?

And if so, a second question. Has the Left lost ground, in significant part, because its earlier postwar success took too exclusively 'realist' and technical a direction, robbing it of both its spirited supporters and its moral vision? That is, has the Left failed to take seriously the demand of its own core commitments to think and act on the basis of moral principle and political vision? If the answer is again yes, then does not the crucial issue become how it might be possible to reconstruct the vision of solidarity and social justice to articulate an attractive as well as a practically viable alternative of democratic community in the era of internationalised capital?

23

© The Political Quarterly Publishing Co. Ltd. 1995.

WILLIAM M. SULLIVAN

The 'growth society': appeal amid dysfunction

It is often noted today that capitalism has developed not the one generic brand long extolled by neoclassical economists and criticised by socialists, but a varied set of forms, shaped by different national polities with their specific histories. In particular, British and American models of 'individualistic' and 'liberal' national capitalisms are distinguished from the more 'communitarian' or 'corporatist' patterns of nations such as Germany or Japan.[1] This reminder of the power of national histories to give particular shape to otherwise universal patterns also sheds useful light upon the international organisation of capitalism as well. It is important to recognise that the international economic regime constructed after 1945 was organised under the aegis of the victorious and enormously powerful United States and largely on American lines.

American liberalism has long aspired to create, at home and abroad if possible, a universal civilisation in which autonomous individuals could freely contract with each other consideringly only their sense of purpose and moral integrity—or self-interest—and the requirements of public order. Supported by advancing technology and propelled by market competition, while freed from historical animosities and irrationalities, this idealised polity would constitute a diffuse system of social cooperation, without commanding central institutions of European type, guided not by state coercion but by the harmonious confluence of enlightened interests.

It is important to realise that this American social ideal, while it places deep confidence in the individual and promotes economic and social competition, does not oppose the individual to community. Rather, individuals are seen as, and urged to become, voluntarily cooperative, while community is understood as an essentially voluntary association which affirms its members' uniqueness, their ability 'to be themselves', while requiring only limited commitment in return. American communities are communities of aspiration. Here individual opportunity is to fund its complement in fellowship with the like-minded, while competitive achievement finds part of its point and much of its significance in voluntary service to the community so understood.

Of the founding ideas of the postwar order, the ideal of ever-widening individual opportunity has proved to be the most influential and long-lasting. Opportunity was understood to be the moral purpose of economic development. Today, with the collapse of the statist economies of the former Soviet sphere along with the Chinese and Indian embrace of unregulated markets, the dream of the growth society is enjoying a second

---

[1] For example, see Lester Thurow, *Going Head To Head: The Upcoming Economic Competition Among Europe, Japan, and the United States*, William Marrow, New York, 1992.

24

© The Political Quarterly Publishing Co. Ltd. 1995.

spring. That dream is deeply rooted in core features of the American polity and culture, especially those features most consonant with philosophical liberalism. While it is by no means coextensive with all of American culture, the concentration upon 'making something of oneself', together with its promise of self-fulfilment in a freely-constructed life has proven deeply appealing. It has also come virtually to define the positive meaning of the United States on the world scene, while it constitutes a large portion of the imaginative aspirations of millions everywhere for the goods of modernity and progress.

These ideals are somewhat more prosaically approximated in American middle-class life. There, for the fortunate, economic opportunity provides the basis for becoming a decent and socially respectable, because contributing, individual, while economic achievement provides the means to enact visions of individual freedom through consumer goods and to enjoy the community of the similarly inclined in lifestyle enclaves.[2] Unfortunately, as an instance of what we might think of as real existing growth society, contemporary American life also reveals the limitations of that ideal. Since it is understood to be a voluntary construction of individuals, the community and its institutions tend to be seen ambivalently. Sometimes, while it seems to serve the ends of growth, the community is an object of devotion and pride, even self-sacrifice. However, the community can also be understood as a set of instrumentalities for the good life, permitting Americans to abandon it—and its less cooperative or successful members—with good conscience when community ties no longer serve to focus the restless quest for progress.

The long-standing and continuing American problem with cities is a case in point. 'Big cities', as historian Sam Bass Warner, Jr. noted during the height of the crisis of the 1960s, 'require habits of community life, an attention to sharing scarce resources, and a willingness to care for all men, not just all successful men, that the American tradition could not fulfil once cities became large and industrialised'.[3] The 'privatism' intrinsic to the American tradition has meant that American society has been willing to tolerate a significantly larger gap in income, health, working and living standards between its more and less successful members than virtually any other.[4] While the Civil Rights movement and the Women's movement put inequalities in a glaring light and opened up significant new channels of opportunity, the weakness of social solidarity has continued to haunt the

[2] See Robert N. Bellah, Richard Madsen, William M. Sullivan, Ann Swiddler, and Steven M. Tipton, *Habits of the Heart: Individualism and Commitment in American Life*, University of California Press, Berkeley and Los Angeles, 1985.

[3] For example, see Sam Bass Warner, Jr., *The Private City: Philadelphia in Three Periods of Its Growth*, University of Pennsylvania Press, Philadelphia, 1968, esp. pp. 84 ff.

[4] For detailed comparisons on this point between the U.S., Sweden, and Great Britain, see David Popenoe, *Private Pleasure, Public Plight: American Metropolitan Community Life in Perspective*, Rutgers University Press, New Brunswick, NJ, 1985.

© The Political Quarterly Publishing Co. Ltd. 1995.

WILLIAM M. SULLIVAN

nation in the form of the despair and violence associated with conditions of inner city poverty.[5]

The negative outcome of short-term strategies

Now, as global economic trends have grown more Darwinian, not only reversing the earlier postwar tendencies toward greater equality, but also placing national economies under ever fiercer competitive pressures, this heritage of privatism has begun to take its toll in the economic heart of the growth system. The growing polarisation of wealth has been accompanied by the spread of 'leaner' but also 'meaner' forms of business organisation. Income, status, and economic security have become even scarcer goods, while distinctions between core and peripheral sectors, regions, enterprises and workers have accelerated markedly everywhere.

The great debate among business and national economic strategies has become the relative merits of investment in the upgrading of skills across the labour force as a whole versus a strategy of suppressing labour costs.[6] The favoured strategy among American corporations, including multinationals, has been to press toward immediate opportunity by shedding workers. Here again, the weakness of a system built around a nearly exclusive attention to opportunity reveals itself, as the press toward immediate economic efficiency can be related directly to deepening problems of social decay which are undermining the stability and morals of the growth society as a whole.

This sort of short-term strategy is today rampant throughout and among the developed nations. But whatever their immediate pay-offs, such strategies inevitably increase the entropy in the system, with negative consequences for the individual participants as well as threatening the viability of the social environment on which they all depend. This is the negative outcome of an interdependence unmediated by trust and solidarity, of the pursuit of opportunity cut loose from the sense of community and the common good. However, no individual strategy, in even the moderately long-run, can escape the logic of interdependence. Either the actors learn to cooperate, submitting their actions to mutual regulation and assuming responsibility for the collective effects of their doings, or they continue to suffer the effects of negative interdependence. How these capacities might in practice be augmented, and the role of politics in this process, is, of course, the critical question.

---

[5] See Cornel West, 'Nihilism In Black America', in *Race Matters*, Beacon, Boston, 1993, pp. 15–32.

[6] See Bennett Harrison, *Lean And Mean: The Changing Landscape of Corporate Power in the Age of Flexibility*, Basic Books, New York, 1994, esp. pp. 3–34; *also* John Goldthorpe, 'The End of Convergence: Corporatist and Dualist Tendencies in Modern Western Societies', in Goldthorpe, ed., *Order and Conflict in Contemporary Capitalism*, Clarendon Press, Oxford, 1984, pp. 315–43. Also see Robert B. Reich, *The Work of Nations: Preparing Ourselves for 21st. Century Capitalism*, Alfred Knopf, New York, 1991.

26

© The Political Quarterly Publishing Co. Ltd. 1995.

The possibilities for democratic civic community

Articulating a convincing alternative to the privatism of the growth society's ideal of 'enterprise culture' must address not only its practical failures, but the attraction of its moral core. An alternative must supply critique; but also acknowledge the real worth of autonomous selfhood and expressive individuality, while giving those values place within a wider, more mature moral vision. Freedom and opportunity are, after all, real and very important moral goods, central to the whole meaning of modern culture. Yet, cultivated as ends in themselves, they remain adolescent and incomplete qualities. Their real value in life, collective as well as individual, depends upon their further integration with other capacities, especially care and responsibility. Only when they become integral parts of a larger web of commitments and relationships can freedom and opportunity attain significance, finding fulfilment as aspects of the larger range of human possibilities within self-sustaining forms of shared life.

Moreover, it is empirically the case that strong yet contributory individuals need strong social bonds of trust and reciprocal loyalties in order to flourish. The theme of communitarianism currently invoked in some sectors of Anglo-American discourse attempts to articulate a version of this idea. In the United States, at least, communitarianism is in the process of trying to give itself political embodiment as a social movement.[7] This alternative to philosophic liberalism as it is ordinarily understood has also begun to receive important support from empirical social investigation in ways which can serve to further the articulation of an alternative to the atomistic viewpoint of the growth society.

These findings give support to the intellectual struggle to reverse some long-standing prejudices of modern social thought, socialist as well as liberal, concerning the priority of the economic and technological 'base' to the 'superstructure' of social relationships and cultural understandings. Specifically, recent historical experience suggests the reversal of the priority, or at least a more complementary view of the relationship between social connectedness and the skills of participation, on the one side, and technology, strategy and technique on the other.

In an important study of Italian regional governments, Robert Putnam has found convincing proof that norms of reciprocity embedded in networks of civic engagement are the critical social conditions which make 'strong, effective, responsive, representative institutions' possible. These same conditions turn out to be key resources for economic as well as political strength.[8] Putnam was able to show that the key difference between regions in which governments operate effectively as compared to

[7] For example, see Amitai Etzioni, *The Spirit of Community: The Reinvention of American Society*, Simon and Schuster, New York, 1993.
[8] Robert D. Putnam, *Making Democracy Work: Civic Traditions in Modern Italy*, Princeton University Press, Princeton, NJ, 1993, pp. 6–8.

© The Political Quarterly Publishing Co. Ltd. 1995.

those in which they remain moribund was the level of what he termed 'civic culture' prevalent in the particular locality.

In the more civic regions, social connections tended to be 'horizontal' more than 'vertical', and 'expectations that others will probably follow the rules' encouraged a general willingness to cooperate. In the less civic regions, the opposite expectations were more common, leading individuals to fulfil everyone's 'dolorous, cynical expectations' that others are not to be trusted (p. 11). The result was more satisfaction with government and with life in the more civic communities, a fatalistic cynicism in the less civic. 'Happiness', Putnam concluded, 'is living in a civic community' (p. 112). In other words, the availability of civic culture made it possible for some regions to escape negative interdependence, while its lack condemned others to suffer its ravages.

The key to social success, Putnam discovered, is the development of moral norms embedded in social networks that work to reduce incentives to defect, reduce uncertainty, and provide models for future cooperation, so that trust is itself an emergent property of the social system as much as a personal attribute (p. 177). In civic regions, the customs which govern everyday life, the norms embedded in a dense network of organisations and associations ranging from political clubs to labour unions to choral societies, simultaneously sponsor enterprise and support concern for the common good. There seemed little need to trade off between economic efficiency and social justice. There, social expectations sanction engagement in public issues, concern for fellow citizens, and a willingness to tolerate differences while working together through a variety of organisations. These shared expectations establish a perspective and sustain a horizon of understanding in which individuals, families, and organisations conceive and pursue their purposes.

By contrast, Putnam found that regions poor in civic practices not only tend to be xenophobic and dependent upon hierarchy and force to control latent social anarchy, but are significantly poorer in material terms as well. A strong civic culture, he discovered, turned out to be the best (in fact, the only strongly significant) predictor of economic success for a locality over the long term. Civic culture, norms and networks of civic engagement seem to be 'the precondition for economic development, as well as for effective government. Development economists take note: civics matters.'[9]

Putnam proposed that the civic and non-civic regions embodied opposite types of socioeconomic 'broad equilibrium' which, once attained, tend to become self-reinforcing. The key differential factor is the presence of community, specified as those norms of reciprocity and networks of civic engagement which Putnam calls social capital. On analogy to economists' use of the term human capital, to refer to those skills which enable individuals to activate the wealth-producing capacities

⁹ Robert C. Putnam, 'The Prosperous Community: Social Capital and Public Life', *The American Prospect*, Number 13, Spring 1993, pp. 35–42; p. 57.

© The Political Quarterly Publishing Co. Ltd. 1995.

of physical capital, social capital is thought of as a moral resource and public good which activates the latent human capital of individuals and populations.[10]

Especially in more complex modern societies, where opportunism can provide such high rewards, social capital becomes more important as enabling networks of trust and interaction to work across great social differentiation and complexity. Thus, Putnam concludes that 'Tocqueville was right', in that effective and responsive formal institutions depend, in the language of civic humanism, on republican virtues and practices (p. 182). Both states and markets work more efficiently—and work more effectively in partnership—in civic settings whose cultural cement is a conception of one's role and obligations as a citizen (p. 183).

It is finally such civic capacities, embedded in a community's practices, which make the difference between negative and positive outcomes of interdependence. Civic culture gives tensile strength and cooperative aims to social relationships. But if so, then the central question of democratic politics becomes more focused. It becomes a question of how a locality can develop as a stronger civic community? Is it possible to achieve a significant level of civic community beyond a city or region, at the level of a whole nation? Finally, what are the implications of such an aim for politics?

Fortunately, Putnam's findings are bolstered and generalised beyond regional Italy and the last two decades by a complementary study of the effects of civic community in the economic affairs of nations. In *Community And The Economy: The Theory of Public Cooperation*, Jonathan Boswell argues for the importance of non-market and non-state processes of social cooperation within and among economic units themselves.[11] This finding is especially important in the face of the pressures now being exerted upon all localities by the anarchic forces of unregulated international capital. The great hope of much modern thought has been the expectation that mutually beneficial exchange would prove a preferred alternative to predatory and exploitative behaviour. Within market systems, this expectation can be subverted and overwhelmed by the power of monopolistic wealth. However, if Boswell is correct, the predatory tendency can be restrained and sublimated towards cooperation from within economic relationships as well as through political controls imposed from without.

Drawing on observations of long-term historical trends running through most of the 20th century, Boswell argues that the most successful national economies over the long run have not been those with the fastest growth rates for any short term, but those which have exhibited the most balanced growth and steady economic performance. Boswell's measure of balance is multifaceted, including steady growth, high employment, low

---

[10] Putnam, *Democracy*, p. 167.
[11] Jonathan Boswell, *Community and the Economy: The Theory of Public Cooperation*, Routledge, London and New York, 1990.

29

© The Political Quarterly Publishing Co. Ltd. 1995.

inflation, avoidance of either major trade deficits or surpluses, the enhancement of a nation's capital assets and physical environment, and at least no worsening of poverty.

According to these measures, Austria, the Benelux countries, Scandinavia, and to a lesser degree Germany, have managed to sustain a high level of long-term investment, considerable planning, and inventiveness in both the public and the private sectors. Most importantly, these countries have been fairly successful in avoiding the economic and social dislocations attendant upon violent 'jerks' in economic policy, swings between reliance upon thrusting market forces which call forth retribution in the form of state coercion which in turn provokes evasion or defiance from a host of buccaneering elements (pp. 164–5). Unhappily, though convincingly, Boswell places the U.K. and U.S.A., in that order, at the bottom of his ranking of states on measures of balanced growth.

The development of this kind of community in the economy has required the nurture over time of highly communicative relations among the sectional interests, including business, labour and education, together with public opinion and governmental entities. Not only the number of participants, but the quality of public cooperation have evolved from often wary consultation to a level of institutionalised participation in national forums in which priorities and goals are debated and established. In polities with a high degree of public cooperation, there is a synergy produced by practices of 'forethought, colloquy and operational adjustment' among economic actors and interested social groupings. The social and political payoffs from these often elaborate and time-consuming practices is 'a diffusion of public tasks, as opposed to these being neglected, centrally monopolized or selfishly defined' (p. 73). Or, in other words, public cooperation signals the transformation of potentially factious economic entities into something like citizens, able and willing to invest their energies in long-term common goals, because they have come to understand themselves as members of national communities.

As he summarises these findings, Boswell emphasises that the development of public cooperation has nowhere been steady nor smooth. It has occurred in what he calls 'decisive upward shifts' precipitated by moments of national emergency. At least equally important, however, has been the availability at these defining moments of widely diffused political ideologies which could give direction to political action. Of particular significance, in Boswell's strong-case societies, were not only social democracy, but also religiously-based conceptions of the common good, such as those promoted by Christian Democrats in the idealistic phases of their movement. Without the presence of such cultural resources, and social groupings committed to their diffusion, nations proved unable to turn emergency into opportunity for fostering higher levels of economic cooperativeness and civic community.

This last point of Boswell's makes explicit a theme implicitly important in Putnam's study as well. Namely, that the very complexity of differentia-

30

© The Political Quarterly Publishing Co. Ltd. 1995.

tion in modern economies makes interdependence harder to grasp, even as it has permitted the expansion of areas of private choice. Under these conditions, not only widely available articulations of visions of economic community, but institutions and movements which attempts to engage citizens and various economic and social groups in 'colloquy' and consultation around such issues may be the crucial resources enabling public cooperation to develop. In a time when social polarisation is increasing across all national economies, this is a very important lesson to assimilate and put into practice.

The menace of multinational capital

One might, however, lodge a major objection to all this. Neither Putnam nor Boswell has included in their pictures the growing menace that multinational capital poses to all efforts at civic community. In other words, however, viable Boswell's lessons may have been within an earlier postwar economic order, they cannot be projected forward into the age of the emerging system. Certainly, from a sceptical point of view it seems utopian to imagine that social solidarity or civic participation can have much to do with the powerful forces at work in the international economy.

In defence of Boswell's position, however, we might note that it continues to seem improbable to many neo-classical economists that these 'soft' factors, whose impact Boswell has documented, can have much to do with levels of employment, production, or prices, or disparities between rich and poor within national economies. In fact, if Boswell is correct about the critical importance of institutions and practices of public cooperation in determining national well-being, then in order to make the 21st century global order humanly tolerable (and politically stable), something resembling transnational civic bonds will have to be constructed.

The global economy, in this extrapolation from the history of national economic development, is now demanding a new level of institutionalisation. If the welfare state of the mid-20th century aimed to buffer national societies and their individual members against the vagaries of the market, the new challenge is to redirect and reform the institutions of public responsibility toward establishing the preconditions for cooperation with civic intent in ways that are both more flexible than the old apparatus and also able to foster linkages across national boundaries, among private and public entities, in the interests of common prosperity and more inclusive well-being.

Taking responsibility for civic community

Community, if the preceding discussion is headed in the right direction, is not simply a moralistic add-on to be attached to serious, 'hard' descriptions of economic processes. Despite the continuing claims of the

31

ideologues of social nominalism, that society is an illusion and only individuals are real, we can point out that the power of community can be seen through its effects. When it is present, as we have seen, all manner of things go well, while in its absence even the state and the market function poorly. Community, like trust, is an emergent property of a well-integrated social organisation. As a social ideal and political purpose, civic community affirms the reciprocal importance of strong individuals and healthy communities. Since individuals become who they are in important measure through their relationships, the upbuilding and nurture of as rich a network of relationships as possible is the best means towards improving the quality of individual life.

Community is also an important political value. It legitimates public attention to and protection of those institutions which, individually and in concert, sustain the health, education, economic opportunity, and social security of citizens, ensuring that each has the means to realise his or her capacities as members of society. This has been the charter of the welfare state. It must again become the charter of an active and responsive civic democracy.

The indispensability of community for democratic citizenship is finally that the experience of community life, by realising the rewards as well as the demands of common life, renders responsibility plausible. Without the practices of communication, trust, and cooperation for common goals according to shared norms which are the stuff of community wherever it is found, the ideals of personal responsibility and public spiritedness must ring hollow or seem superhuman ideals. Community life, which is always in the last resort tied to place and history, is the context in which the character of citizens is formed. Only if this base is generally intact and available for most citizens can individuals go on to expand the spirit of public responsibility in forms appropriate to larger-scale organisations and, hopefully, developing transnational institutions of cooperation as well.

Civic community makes possible dimensions of experience not available to individuals in more meanly endowed moral environments. As part of a functioning civic community, individuals can transcend their own limitations, even to some degree their very mortality, by affirming and serving the good of that community as their own. This is because each knows that, while dependent upon others and their cooperation for their very survival, each is also reminded in a hundred small ways that he or she is maintaining the whole as well, that the community is in important ways committed to the individual's care. Since the relationship is thus reciprocal, citizens can affirm themselves in service to the whole community and the values for which it stands. The life of the community, for its part, by surpassing and outlasting individuals, also gives them identity, significance, and a final vindication.

© The Political Quarterly Publishing Co. Ltd. 1995.

© The Political Quarterly Publishing Co. Ltd. 1995. Published by Blackwell Publishers, 108 Cowley Road, Oxford
OX4 1JF, UK and 238 Main Street, Cambridge, MA 02142, USA.

ECONOMIC POLICY FOR ENVIRONMENTAL SUSTAINABILITY

PAUL EKINS*

'Unrestrained resource consumption for energy production and other uses
... could lead to catastrophic outcomes for the global environment. Some of
the environmental changes may produce irreversible damage to the earth's
capacity to sustain life. ... The future of our planet is in the balance.' [UK
Royal Society & US National Academy of Sciences, 1992, pp. 2, 4.]

DURING the last twenty years an increasingly pronounced scientific consensus on the environmental unsustainability of current human ways of
life has emerged, with the consensus being politically endorsed by the 176
countries whose governments were represented at the Earth Summit in
1992 in Rio de Janeiro.

What the government actually signed up to in Rio was a concept called
'sustainable development', a term which was at the core of *The Rio
Declaration on Environment and Development*[1] (pp. 11–13) and of
Agenda 21, which called for 'a global partnership for sustainable development', with sustainable development taking on the character of the
ultimate wish-list, entailing 'the fulfilment of basic needs, improved living
standards for all, better protected and managed ecosystems and a safer,
more prosperous future' (p. 47).

Sustainable development had been the flagship concept of the
Brundtland Report,[2] but soon came to mean many different things to
different people. By 1989 Pearce *et al.*[3] (pp. 173–85) were able to cite a
'gallery of definitions', which by 1994 could have been much extended. To
Lele[4] (p. 613) 'Sustainable development is a "meta-fix" that will unite

* Paul Ekins is a Research Fellow at the Department of Economics, Birkbeck College,
London, and a Research Associate at the Department of Applied Economics at the
University of Cambridge, analysing the relationship between environmental sustainability,
energy use and economic growth. He is the author of *A New World Order*, Routledge, 1992;
and co-editor of *Real-Life Economics*, Routledge, 1992 and *Global Warming and Energy
Demand*, Routledge, 1994.

[1] *Earth Summit '92*, Regency Press, London.
[2] WCED (World Commission on Environment and Development), *Our Common Future*
(The Brundtland Report), Oxford University Press, Oxford/New York, 1987.
[3] D. Pearce, A. Markandya, E. Barbier, *Blueprint for a Green Economy*, Earthscan,
London, 1989.
[4] S. Lele, 'Sustainable Development: a Critical Review', *World Development*, Vol. 19,
No. 6, 1991, pp. 607–21.

everybody'. To Beckermann[5] (p. 491) 'It is far from clear what concept of "sustainable development" can be both morally acceptable and operationally meaningful'.

Part of the definitional problem clearly arises from the composite nature of the concept of sustainable development, involving both 'development' and 'sustainability'. Now the debate about what constitutes development has a considerable history which has spawned an enormous literature, which cannot be even perfunctorily examined here. For present purposes it is enough to characterise development as a process which results in the increased welfare of the group under consideration, with special reference to the least well-off members of the group.

Other things being equal, increases in *per capita* income may be considered to contribute positively to development, but clearly many other factors are also contributors to human welfare, including health, education, income distribution, employment, working conditions, leisure, environmental quality and security, social cohesion and spiritual coherence. There is no numeraire that can evaluate the trade-offs between these various factors, so that at a time when some are changing for the better and others for the worse it becomes very difficult to say whether 'development' is taking place or not.

For example, it is debatable whether the UK is more 'developed' than it was twenty or thirty years ago. Table 1 shows that its GDP was certainly much higher in 1991 than in 1971, having grown by 46 per cent. But unemployment is also much higher, there is less job security, income distribution is more unequal, the poorest people have benefited least from growth, in relative as well as absolute terms, and there is more violence, crime and family breakdown. With regard to the environment, one conclusion on the basis of a recent set of measures was 'in many areas the UK environment is in "poor condition", and in some cases the situation is actually deteriorating'[6] (p. 76); globally damage continues at a high rate to such resources as forests and fisheries and significant new global threats to the atmosphere have emerged. Such considerations led one calculation of Sustainable Economic Welfare in the UK to conclude: 'Welfare in the UK has not improved over the study period [1950–1990] at anything like the rate that a conventional measure of GNP would have us believe. In particular, sustainable economic welfare appears to have declined in this country since the mid-1970s'[7] (p. 36).

The weighing of such complex issues, and the striving for balance between them, is the stuff of democratic politics and political debate, of

[5] W. Beckermann, 'Economic Growth and the Environment: Whose Growth? Whose Environment?', *World Development*, Vol. 20, No. 4, pp. 481–96.

[6] ECG (Environment Challenge Group), *Environmental Measures: Indicators for the UK Environment*, ECG, London, 1994. (Also available from New Economics Foundation, London.)

[7] T. Jackson and N. Marks, *Measuring Sustainable Economic Welfare—A Pilot Index: 1950–1990*, Stockholm Environment Institute, Stockholm, 1994.

34

© The Political Quarterly Publishing Co. Ltd. 1995.

course, so that it is hardly surprising that the 'development' component of sustainable development remains contested and confusing ground. But the same is not true of the 'sustainability' component of the term, which is increasingly coming to be the organising principle of public policy with regard to the environment. This paper sets out the basic dimensions and parameters of sustainability and relates them to

TABLE 1   HAS THE UK BECOME MORE 'DEVELOPED'
FROM 1961-91?

	1991	1981	1971	1961
Gross domestic product (GDP)[1]				
(£1985 billion)	345	275	236	183
Unemployment, %[2]	8.7	9.8	3.3	1.3
Income per week:	(1993)			
Bottom tenth:[3]				
Amount (£1993)	175		138	
Index	127		100	
Top tenth:				
Amount (£1993)	567		336	
Index	169		100	
Net income, %[4]	(1990-1)		(1973)	
Bottom fifth	7	10	8	
Top fifth	41	36	37	
Recorded offences	(1991)		(1971)	
(thousands):[5]				
Violence against the person	190	100	47	17
Sexual offences	29	19	24	15
Burglary	1219	718	452	na[6]
Families headed by lone			(1976)	
parents, %[7]	18	12	10	
Divorces			(1971)	
(thousands)[8]	171	156	79	27

[1] At factor cost. The 1971, 1981 figures come from *UK National Income and Expenditure (UKNIE) 1991* (HMSO, London), Table 1.1, pp. 10–11; the 1991 figure comes from *UKNIE 1994*, Table 1.1, pp. 10–11, converted from £1990 to £1985; the 1961 figure from *UKNIE 1974*, Table 8, pp. 10–11, converted from the index number series.
[2] The 1981, 1991 figures come from *Social Trends (ST) 1994* (HMSO, London), Table 4.19, p. 62; the 1961, 1971 figures come from *ST 1984*, Table 4.16, p. 66.
[3] The bottom tenth figure is the maximum amount earned by men in that part of the income distribution; the top tenth figure is the minimum amount earned by men in that part of the distribution. Figures from *ST 1994*, Table 5.5, p. 69.
[4] Before housing costs. Figures from *ST 1994*, Table 5.20, p. 77.
[5] England & Wales. Figures for 1981, 1991 from *ST 1994*, Table 12.2, p. 152; for 1971 from *ST 1984*, Table 12.1, p. 165; for 1961, *ST 1974*, Table 169, p. 187.
[6] Recorded under different categories.
[7] Figures from *ST 1994*, Table 2.8, p. 36.
[8] Figures from *ST 1994*, Table 2.13, p. 38.

© The Political Quarterly Publishing Co. Ltd. 1995.

processes of wealth-creation. It shows how the concept of sustainability can be made politically operational and explores some of the implications of this for economic policy and public policy more generally.

Environmental sustainability: definitions and determinants

The basic meaning of sustainability is the capacity for continuance more or less indefinitely into the future. It is now clear that, in aggregate, current human ways of life do not possess that capacity, either because they are destroying the environmental conditions necessary for their continuance, or because their environmental effects will cause unacceptable social disruption and damage to human health. The environmental effects in question include climate change, ozone depletion, acidification, toxic pollution, the depletion of renewable resources (e.g. forests, soils, fisheries, water) and of non-renewable resources (e.g. fossil fuels) and the extinction of species.

A way of life is a complex bundle of values, objectives, institutions and activities, with ethical, environmental, economic and social dimensions. While current concern about unsustainability largely has an ecological basis, it is clear that human situations or ways of life can be unsustainable for social and economic reasons as well. The pertinent questions are: for the environment, can its contribution to human welfare and to the human economy be sustained? for the economy, can today's level of wealth-creation be sustained? and for society, can social cohesion and important social institutions be sustained?

Provided that the inter-relatedness of the different dimensions is borne in mind, it can be useful to distinguish between the implications for sustainability of human mores, relationships and institutions (the social dimension); of the allocation and distribution of scarce resources (the economic dimension); and of the contribution to both of these from, and their effects on, the environment and its resources (the ecological dimension). Clearly human relationships may be socially unsustainable (for example, those leading to civil war) independently of economic or ecological factors; and a particular allocation of resources may be economically unsustainable (leading, for example, to growing budget deficits) independently of social or ecological factors. Similarly, a given level of economic growth may be unsustainable for purely economic reasons, in so far as it is leading to increased inflation or balance of payments deficits; on the other hand, it may be socially unsustainable in so far as it is increasing income inequalities or undermining structures of social cohesion such as the family or community; or it may be environmentally unsustainable in so far as it is depleting resources on which the economic growth itself depends.

One way of illustrating the complexities involved is through the matrix shown in Table 2, where the rows show the types of sustainability, and the

36

columns the influence on those types, across the same dimensions. In the example above, the sustainability of economic growth would be considered across the second row, with environmental influences (e.g. resource depletion) in box A, economic influences (e.g. inflation, balance of payments) in box B, and social influences (e.g. social cohesion) in box C. A fourth column has been added to the matrix to indicate the importance for sustainability of ethical influences. Relevant influences in box E, for example, would be concern for future generations or non-human forms of life; in box F they could be attitudes to poverty and income distribution.

TABLE 2 TYPES OF SUSTAINABILITY AND THEIR INTERACTIONS

Types of Sustainability	Influences on Sustainability			
	Ethical	Environmental	Economic	Social
Environmental	E		D	
Economic		A	B	C
Social	F			

Environmental sustainability may always be considered a desirable characteristic of a human situation, though some states of such sustainability may be better than others. In contrast, economic and social sustainability have no such happy connotation. As Hardoy *et al.* stress: 'When judged by the length of time for which they (were) sustained, some of the most successful societies were also among the most exploitative, where the abuse of human rights was greatest'[8] (pp. 180–1). Also, poverty and the evils which go with it may be all too sustainable. Similarly, in many countries structural unemployment is showing worrying signs of long-term sustainability.

My principal focus is the environment-economy relationship (i.e. Boxes A, D in Table 2). But such a focus necessarily includes all the above dimensions, the implications of which for environmental sustainability will be briefly explored later in this chapter.

Understanding wealth-creation

Economic activity creates wealth by combining different factors of production in order to produce goods and services. The means of combination of a particular production process is that process's technology. Production can increase either when the quantities of the factor increase,

---

[8] J. Hardoy, D. Mitlin, D. Satterthwaite, *Environmental Problems in Third World Cities*, Earthscan, London, 1993.

37

© The Political Quarterly Publishing Co. Ltd. 1995.

or when they are combined more effectively so that the same factors produce more output. The latter condition is called technical change.

There are three distinct factors of production, which may be thought of as three types of capital, as portrayed in Figure 1: ecological (or natural) capital, human (individual and social) capital, and manufactured capital. Each of these stocks produces a flow of 'services'—environmental, E, labour, L, and capital, K—which serve as inputs into the productive process, along with 'intermediate inputs', M, which are previous outputs from the economy which are used as inputs in a subsequent process.

Manufactured capital comprises material goods—tools, machines, buildings, infrastructure—which contribute to the production process but do not become embodied in the output and, usually, are 'consumed' in a period of time longer than a year. Intermediate goods, in contrast, either are embodied in produced goods (e.g. metals, plastics, components) or are immediately consumed in the productive process (e.g. fuels). Human capital comprises all individuals' capacities for work (skills, knowledge, health, strength, motivation) and the networks and organisations through which they are mobilised.

Ecological capital is a complex category which performs three distinct types of environmental function, two of which are directly relevant to the production process. The first is the provision of resources for production, the raw materials that become food, fuels, metals, timber etc. The second is the absorption of wastes from production, both from the production process and from the disposal of consumption goods. Where these wastes add to or improve the stock of ecological capital (e.g. through recycling or fertilisation of soil by livestock), they can be regarded as investment in such capital. More frequently, where they destroy, pollute or erode, with consequent negative impacts on the ecological, human or manufactured capital stocks, they can be regarded as agents of negative investment, depreciation or capital consumption.

The third type of environmental function does not contribute directly to production, but in many ways it is the most important type because it provides the basic context and conditions within which production is possible at all. It comprises basic 'survival services', such as those producing climate and ecosystem stability, shielding of ultraviolet radiation by the ozone layer; and 'amenity services', such as the beauty of wilderness and other natural areas. These services are produced directly by ecological capital independently of human activity, but human activity can certainly have an (often negative) effect on the responsible capital and therefore on the services produced by it.

The outputs of the economic process can, in the first instance, be categorised as 'Goods' and 'Bads'. The Goods are the desired outputs of the process, as well as any positive externalities (incidental effects) that may be associated with it. These Goods can be divided in turn into consumption, investment and intermediate goods and services. The Bads are the negative effects of the production process, including capital

38

© The Political Quarterly Publishing Co. Ltd. 1995.

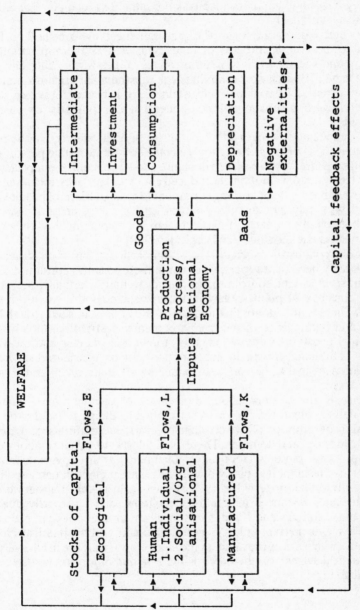

FIGURE 1   Stocks, Flows and Welfare in the Process of Production

39

© The Political Quarterly Publishing Co. Ltd. 1995.

depreciation and negative externalities, such as those contributing to environmental destruction, negative effects on human health etc. In so far as they have an effect on the capital stocks, the Bads can be regarded as negative investment.

To some extent, one form of capital can substitute for another. It is possible to view the process of industrialisation as the application of human and social capital to natural capital to transform it into human-made capital. But it is now clear that such substitutability is not complete. If our current development is unsustainable, it is because it is depleting some critical, non-substitutable components of the capital base on which it depends.

The goods and services which comprise or, equivalently, can be purchased with, a person's or a nation's income contribute to that person's or nation's welfare. Welfare is seen in Figure 1 to be affected by many factors apart from the consumption of produced goods and services, including the process of production (working conditions), the institutions of production (the firm, family, community, political/legal system), people's state of health (part of human capital) and environmental quality (negative externalities and the stock of ecological capital).

Western industrial societies are often called 'consumer societies', presumably because it is perceived that in these societies consumption is the most important contributor to human welfare. Certainly, the principal objective of public policy in these societies is the growth of the GNP. There is little doubt that in the past and at present such growth has been and is the cause of much environmental destruction. One of the principal questions raised by such destruction is whether and on what terms continuing growth in consumption can be considered environmentally sustainable, i.e. can be sustained by the environment in the long term.

There is no mystery about the causes of current environmental degradation, which can be squarely ascribed to the patterns of production and consumption of five economic sectors: energy, industry, agriculture, transport and tourism. There is similarly no mystery about the reasons why these sectors have operated in an environmentally destructive fashion. It is partly due to the fact that environmental effects frequently remain external to the price mechanism that registers costs and allocates resources in a market economy; and it is partly due to ignorance, complacency and short-termism in the political process. Remedying the market-failures, on the one hand, and the political short-comings, which are as prevalent in the electorate as they are in all levels of the political system, on the other, is the *sine qua non* of moves towards sustainability.

© The Political Quarterly Publishing Co. Ltd. 1995.

Environmental sustainability: making the concept operational

For environmental sustainability to become an operational concept, it must be defined in terms of physical conditions or imperatives, such as the following:

- Destabilisation of global environmental features such as climate patterns or the ozone layer must be prevented;
- Important ecosystems and ecological features must be absolutely protected to maintain biological diversity;
- Renewable resources must be renewed through the maintenance of soil fertility, hydrobiological cycles and necessary vegetative cover. Sustainable harvesting must be rigorously enforced;
- Depletion of non-renewable resources should seek to balance the maintenance of a minimum life-expectancy of the resources with the development of substitutes for it. Once the minimum life-expectancy had been reached, consumption of the resources would have to be matched by new discoveries of it. To help finance research for alternatives and the eventual transition to renewal substitutes, all depletion of non-renewable resources should entail a contribution to a capital fund. The need to minimise the depletion of all but the most abundant non-renewable resources implies that these resources should be used as intensively as possible by designing for resource-efficiency, durability and the maximum feasible practice of repair, reconditioning, re-use and recycling (the 'four R's');
- Emissions into air, soil and water must not exceed their critical load, that is the capability of the receiving media to disperse, absorb, neutralise and recycle them, nor may they lead to life-damaging concentrations of toxins;
- Risks of life-damaging events from human activity must be kept at very low levels. Technologies, such as nuclear power, which threaten long-lasting ecosystem damage at whatever level of risk, should be foregone.

The actual physical standards which are consistent with these conditions will derive largely from the natural sciences, with application of the Precautionary Principle in situations of uncertainty.[9] These standards could serve as a framework of indicators of sustainability, comprising a set of physical criteria that offer as far as possible a guarantee of ecosystem diversity, health, stability and resilience, from the local to the global level. Much detailed research on these indicators is ongoing (see, for example, ECG, *op. cit.*).

Humans today are part of most ecosystems in the biosphere. Through their quest for welfare and development, they exert an influence on all of

---

[9] See for example, T. O'Riordan, 'Interpreting the Pre-cautionary Principle', CSERGE Working Paper PA 93–01, CSERGE, University of East Anglia, Norwich, 1993.

41

© The Political Quarterly Publishing Co. Ltd. 1995.

them. Their activities proceed from complex motivations in pursuit of diverse goals and are promoted, mediated and constrained by a dense web of institutions and cultural relations at a variety of levels, all of which must be understood if policies directed towards the achievement of sustainability, as defined by the indicator framework, are to be effectively implemented.

The extent to which societies are and will be prepared to move towards sustainability depends not only on the value they place on the concept *per se*, but also on their situation: their ambitions, perceived realities, opportunities and constraints. If analysis and policy formulation are to help or persuade societies to become more sustainable, they will need to be located in a multi-dimensional understanding of this situation, so that ambitions and perceived realities can be appropriately changed, constraints lifted and opportunities taken.

The ethics of sustainability

'Even the narrow notion of physical sustainability implies a concern for social equity between generations, a concern that must logically be extended to equity within each generation. ... Our inability to promote the common interest in sustainable development is often a product of the relative neglect of economic and social justice within and amongst nations.' [WCED, *op. cit.*, pp. 43, 49.]

'The ethical imperative of stewardship ... must underlie all environmental policies. ... We have a moral duty to look after our planet and hand it on in good order to future generations.' [HMG,[10] p. 10.]

How a society uses its environment depends first and foremost on its world view, its perception of the nature of the world and the status of human beings and other life forms within it. It is likely, for example, that a secular, anthropocentric world view will sanction different uses of the environment, and permit more environmental destruction, than one in which the earth and all life within it is perceived as sacred.

From its world view a society will derive its concept of environmental justice: the relative rights of non-human forms of life, of future human generations, and of current human generations to benefit from, share or just exist in 'the environment'. Environmental sustainability gains in strength as an imperative the more it is perceived that the well-being and opportunities of future humans and non-human beings should not be sacrificed for present human advantage.

From its world view, too, a society will derive its means for valuing and taking decisions about the environment. If the environment is viewed primarily as an economic resource, then techniques of environmental economic valuation will be perceived as the most important environmental inputs into decision-making processes.

It is likely that a society's norms of environmental justice will be related

---

[10] HM Government, *This Common Inheritance*, HMSO, London, 1990.

42

© The Political Quarterly Publishing Co. Ltd. 1995.

to its norms of economic and social justice. If basic personal and civil rights are denied, then environmental rights are unlikely to be respected, or even recognised. Thus sustainability and democracy are related. Further, if non-environmental economic wealth is unequally distributed, access to environmental goods is also likely to be inegalitarian. This has an obvious and direct importance for sustainability, if indeed it is true that poverty is a great destroyer of the environment, as is often asserted.

The ethics of sustainability will also determine to a considerable extent where the responsibility for promoting environmental sustainability is perceived to lie, and the degree of coercion in its enforcement that is considered justified. The Polluter Pays Principle, acceded to by OECD countries as early as 1972, but as much or more honoured in the breach as in the observance, is not only a maxim of economic efficiency; it is also a statement of moral responsibility. If polluters under prevailing economic and social arrangements do not pay, and governments are invoked to make them do so, how governments proceed with this task will depend on the political and social contract between governors and governed, on balances of rights and responsibilities and the institutions that express and enforce them. This leads naturally to consideration of sustainability's social dimension.

The social dimension of sustainability

'Critical to the effective implementation of the objectives, policies, and mechanisms ... of *Agenda 21* will be the commitment and genuine involvement of all social groups.' [*Agenda 21*, Chapter 23, Preamble, *Earth Summit '92, op. cit.*, p. 191.]

Social sustainability refers to a society's ability to maintain, on the one hand, the necessary means of wealth-creation to reproduce itself and, on the other, a shared sense of social purpose to foster social integration and cohesion. Partly this is a question of having a sustainable economy, as discussed below. Partly it is a question of culture and values. Social sustainability is likely to be a necessary condition for the widespread commitment and involvement which *Agenda 21* sees as critical to the achievement of sustainable development.

The importance that Western 'consumer' societies attach to consumption is not only problematic environmentally, because of the level of consumption, and consequent environmental impacts, to which such an emphasis leads. It is also problematic socially. A dominant social goal of increasing individualistic consumption does not seem likely to foster social cohesion, especially in an economic system that is subject to cyclical recession and increasing inequality. Poverty is always an economic problem in the sense that it denotes chronic scarcity at an individual level. It is an ethical problem because this scarcity often induces acute suffering. In some industrialised countries, relative (and sometimes absolute) poverty is also a growing social problem, in terms of its impacts on the

43

© The Political Quarterly Publishing Co. Ltd. 1995.

social fabric and on the social sense of security, which act to reduce the well-being of the non-poor.

The sense of identity and social purpose of very many people, as well as their income, derives in large part from their employment. Extended unemployment, therefore, not only leads to poverty, but also to the loss of these other characteristics, which is probably more to blame than poverty for unemployment's high correlation with ill-health, mental stress and family breakdown. Unemployment is not just a waste of economic resources, in terms of the unemployed's lost production. It is socially destructive as well, and, at levels not much higher than those presently pertaining in Europe, may be expected to be socially unsustainable. Welfare states were established, both to give practical expression to a sense of social justice and to maintain social cohesion, at far lower levels of unemployment. At current levels they find it difficult to sustain the necessary transfer payments to accomplish these objectives, especially in a climate of growing international competition and taxpayer resistance.

Another contributor to people's sense of identity is their membership of and involvement in their local community. In an era of globalisation, the economic life of local communities tends to become increasingly extended. The concept of a local economy that contributes to local liveli-hoods and responds to local priorities is increasingly unrealistic. To a lesser extent, even national economic options are becoming externally determined. Yet the principal political institutions, that are expected to promote wealth-creation and foster wider well-being, operate at the national and sub-national level. Globalisation damages a sense of social connectedness, of community, while the mismatch between economic and political realities undermines confidence in political processes. Neither phenomenon is helpful for social sustainability. It is possible that local environmental action—both political and practical—will help to maintain or regenerate local social purpose and identity.

Such considerations demand that policies and initiatives for promoting an environmentally sustainable economy—by which, as earlier defined, is meant a system and processes of wealth-creation that can be projected to continue well into the future—be located securely within the context that recognises and seeks to address other social priorities and concerns. Policy integration for environmental sustainability does not only mean assessing and improving environmental outcomes over the whole range of policymaking. It also means implementing environmental policy in a way that, as far as possible, is consistent with and contributes to the achieve-ment of society's non-environmental objectives. A trajectory towards environmental sustainability that unnecessarily violates other social priorities is unlikely itself to be sustainable. Attempts to promote such a trajectory may bring the whole project of environmental sustainability into disrepute.

© The Political Quarterly Publishing Co. Ltd. 1995.

Towards a sustainable economy

'The ability to anticipate and prevent environmental damage requires that the ecological dimensions of policy be considered at the same time as the economic, trade, energy, agricultural and other dimensions.' [WCED, *op. cit.*, p. 10.]

The achievement of the integration of environmental policy with other policy areas was a key objective of the UK Government's White Paper on the Environment (*op. cit.*, p. 230). In the event, this objective has proved difficult to realise in practice and the UK environment continues to be adversely affected by policies in other areas, such as transport and agriculture. The following points briefly discuss the range of issues which link the environment and the economy.

Macroeconomic management: narrow economic sustainability, in the sense of broadly balanced budgets and trade flows, is an essential prerequisite of moves towards environmental sustainability. Neither inflation nor indebtedness—public, private or foreign—will be conducive to the implementation of necessary environmental policies. Such policies must never lose sight of the need for macroeconomic stability.

Growth and environment: both the sign and scale of the relationship between the growth of national income and environmental sustainability are variable. There are many opportunities for improving the environment that will also have positive economic impacts. There are also many environmentally destructive activities that will have to be transformed or reduced. The imperative for environmental policy is to realise the win-win opportunities; and to transform or reduce destructive activities in ways that minimise adjustment costs and create new competitive advantages. The available evidence indicates that giving priority to environmental sustainability need not reduce incomes from current levels; it may not even reduce growth. But there is no doubt that it will require economically acute and politically sensitive handling of radical change.

Trade and environment: UK national environmental policymaking is constrained by treaty commitments to both the European Union and the General Agreement on Tariffs and Trade, now the World Trade Organisation. The extent to which these constraints need to be modified or constrained if countries are to be able to promote environmental sustainability is now a major issue of current debate. So is the extent to which the current trading rules' emphasis on non-discrimination and multilateralism can or should be modified to take more account of human rights, labour standards or the specific welfare and development of low income countries. Striking the right balance between these objectives is of crucial importance to sustainability.

Ecological footprints: quite apart from the way trading rules constrain national environmental policymaking, trade often involves the import and export of sustainability. When the production processes of imported

45

© The Political Quarterly Publishing Co. Ltd. 1995.

goods cause environmental impacts, then the importing country may be said to have left its ecological footprint in the goods' country of origin. Policies to move a country towards sustainability must address its ecological footprints abroad.

Sustainability and development: environmental unsustainability is a planetary phenomenon and is likely to continue for as long as large numbers of people live in absolute poverty and try to extricate themselves from this situation by following the Western model of industrial development through the exploitation and consequent destruction of natural resources. Perhaps the most important role of the West in moving towards sustainability is to embark on a new path of development that does not entail environmental destruction. But the West will also need to help lower income countries embark on such a path in a way that is appropriate for them. Environmentally sustainable trade and foreign direct investment will play their role in this, but there will also be a need for aid for sustainable development, and for the foreign indebtedness of many countries to be reduced. The environmental record of aid is not generally good, and any alleviation of debt will have to ensure that further unsustainable indebtedness is not contracted. Renewed North-South cooperation will be necessary to address these issues.

Environmental accounting and valuation: it is generally accepted that the first priority for effective environmental policy is a comprehensive system of environmental accounts across all the environment's relevant dimensions, which gives a clear picture of the state of the environment and changes in this state over time. There is less consensus over how this state and these changes should be valued. In an economistic society it will be easier to incorporate non-market environmental effects into decision-making processes if they can be given a monetary value. The techniques of such valuation therefore have an important role. One such technique, calculating the restoration cost of environmental damage or depletion incurred in a particular period of time, allows the national accounts to be adjusted for environmental factors. Both the United Nations Statistical Office and the European Commission's Fifth Environmental Action Programme now recommend that this should be done. Where monetary valuation of environmental effects is either not possible or not perceived as appropriate, the relative effects should still be considered in decisions.

Ecological tax reform: current taxes bear most heavily on labour. Profits are also taxed. Environmental factors of production, whether resources or waste-absorption services, are hardly taxed at all. Such a taxation system increases the economy's use of the environment, decreases its use of labour and discourages entrepreneurial initiative relative to an untaxed economy. It is hard to justify such a system in a society with worrying levels of both unemployment and environmental damage and which wishes to stimulate enterprise. A shift of taxation away from labour and profits onto the use of environmental resources could be expected to increase investment and employment and reduce environmental damage. Such a shift is

46

© The Political Quarterly Publishing Co. Ltd. 1995.

probably the largest single source of win-win opportunity in the search for sustainability with prosperity.

Environment and employment: ecological tax reform will promote employment both by making labour less expensive relative to other factors of production and by increasing the demand of labour-intensive economic sectors. There is little prospect, however, that it will 'solve' the present unemployment problem. Social sustainability demands that this problem, especially with regard to long-term unemployment and unemployment concentrated in particular age-groups, ethnic minorities or areas, be addressed by a range of other measures, including the redeployment of benefit payments, training, the enhancement of competitiveness, local economic initiatives and environmental works. The formulation and implementation of a successful combination of these measures will not be easy.

Instruments of environmental policy: it is imperative for sustainability that environmental policy objectives are achieved at least cost. It is well-established that market-based incentives are most likely to achieve this. Allied to the Polluter Pays Principle, these will normally take the form of environmental taxes or charges. Such an approach meshes well with the broader objective of ecological tax reform, as discussed above. It will also be the case, however, that environmental policy objectives will sometimes be best achieved by combining market-based instruments with more traditional environmental regulations; and sometimes regulations by themselves will be appropriate. Prior ideological preference has little role to play in choosing the best mix of instruments. Careful analysis of appropriateness on a case-by-case basis is the only way that least-cost sustainability will be approached.

Environment and planning: because markets for many economically important environmental functions are either missing or imperfect, planning has a crucial role to play in policy for sustainability. This applies not only to land-use planning but also to policies for pollution emissions and resource depletion. It remains generally true, however, that least-cost moves towards sustainability will be achieved when planning works with rather than against the grain of the market. Sometimes market pressures will need to be resisted; but environmental policy will be most easily and cost-effectively implemented when market-forces can be guided and redirected rather than simply thwarted. Planning will also generally be most effectively achieved when it proceeds through a process of in-depth consultation and partnership-in-implementation with those parties affected by planning proposals, especially local communities.

Subsidies and environmental investment: it is a fundamental insight of environmental economics that ecological costs are as real as any other category of economic costs. Many such costs are increased by the financial subsidising of environmentally damaging activities, such as energy use or agriculture. Because subsidies also introduce economic inefficiency, removing those that are linked to environmental destruction provides

47

© The Political Quarterly Publishing Co. Ltd. 1995.

another means of securing both economic and environmental gain. Similarly, environmental benefits are as real as any other economic benefits, and the cost of securing them should therefore be regarded as investment rather than consumption. There is a need for methodologies to be developed and deployed that will permit the rate of return on such environmental investments to be quantified, in monetary terms if possible, so that the full benefits of environmental expenditures may be apparent.

Environment and technology: technical change is the driving force of an economy. In the past much of such change has been damaging to the environment. These technologies will have to be transformed or abandoned. In the future technology has the potential to produce humanity's goods and services at a small fraction of their current environmental cost. The development and widespread diffusion of such technologies, in both North and South, is one of the priorities and prerequisites of sustainable development.

Environment and competitiveness: in an increasingly competitive global market economy, there is a limit to the extent to which a country can unilaterally impose environmental costs on its businesses. There are three ways in which environmental policy can be implemented without either running counter to the imperatives of competitiveness or involving unilaterally conceived and imposed protectionism: through global environmental agreements that impose the same (or acceptably differing) constraints on all parties; through agreements brokered, for example, by the World Trade Organisation, that countries can compensate their firms for expensive environmental regulations; and through the use of environmental policy to foster new sources of competitiveness. Each of these ways will be appropriate in different situations. One of them always needs to be politically feasible if the need to compete is not to become the enemy of sustainability.

Environment and consumption: greatly increased levels of consumption are an undisputed cause of global environmental damage. To remedy this situation, either the same goods will have to be produced, used and disposed of differently (with greatly reduced environmental damage); or different goods, which inherently involve less environmental damage, will have to be consumed; or fewer goods will have to be consumed. Sustainable development is likely to require all three remedies in some combination. The first is the least problematic politically, but requires the necessary technical fix; the second depends on changing preferences, through a change in either values or relative prices; the third would become politically less daunting if there were general public recognition of what much survey data reveal: that most people do not regard increasing their consumption as the principal objective or source of satisfaction in their lives. With such recognition, the need on occasion to sacrifice material consumption for socio-environmental benefits would be a politically less problematic message. It will also be important to foster and harness consumer awareness and commitment through appropriate

48

© The Political Quarterly Publishing Co. Ltd. 1995.

labelling schemes that allow the environmentally preferable products in their fields to be identified. Life-cycle analysis will play an important role in providing the scientific foundations of such schemes.

Environment and cities: by the end of the century about half of the world's population will live in large urban settlements, with the proportion still growing. Cities can promote economic dynamism. They can also offer important opportunities for environmental economies of scale. But they can also constitute a major source of environmental problems. Achieving compatibility of cities and sustainability is an important requirement of sustainable development.

Environment, community and the local economy: in the global market-place the very concept of a local economy may appear, and to some extent is, anomalous. But 'environment' will always to a large extent be experienced locally and, as a major contributor to economic welfare, it is important to the local community and part of a local economy. Local initiative is essential to local environmental conservation and enhancement. However, in areas on the periphery of, or otherwise badly served by, the global economy, it will not be easy to mobilise this initiative unless it is linked to efforts at economic regeneration. The creation of environmentally sustainable local economic activity is a key component of sustainable development in such areas. Local government has an important role to play in the promotion of such activity, in the development of more sustainable ways to deliver local services, and in the stimulation of local environmental awareness and commitment. The extent to which UK local authorities, coordinated through the Local Agenda 21 Committee convened by the Local Government Management Board, have responded to UNCED's call for integrated local action for sustainable development represents one of the most positive outcomes of the Rio Summit. Whether through fostering public-private-voluntary sector partnerships, or taking their own initiatives where appropriate, local authorities have a key role in building the local commitment and institutions to undertake the transition to sustainability. The Local Agenda 21 process should be given effective support.

Environment and the welfare state: it is widely acknowledged that the welfare state in the UK and in other industrialised countries faces formidable challenges from a combination of taxpayer resistance and the need for competitiveness, on the one hand, and, on the other, from growing demands from an ageing population, high expectations for health care, expanding education and training needs and persistently high levels of unemployment. Together with growing job insecurity, the pressures on the welfare state increase a sense of social anxiety and insecurity overall, making more difficult the achievement of settled, long-term environmental commitment that is necessary for progress towards sustainability. Resolving the crisis of the welfare state—finding affordable means to enable all people to secure satisfying work, health for all and dignified retirement—is therefore an important objective for environmental as well

49

© The Political Quarterly Publishing Co. Ltd. 1995.

as social sustainability. However, the extent to which moves towards environmental sustainability alone can mitigate the welfare state's problem of financial unsustainability should not be over-emphasised. But there are relevant connections. Unemployment coexists with large amounts of environmental work that needs to be done. Pollution causes ill-health at the same time as health budgets are under stress. A cleaner, safer environment would save substantial costs which currently fall upon the public sector. Major programmes of public environmental works could reduce unemployment. Where, as with energy conservation, they contribute to more efficient resource use, they may involve small, or even negative, costs. Where they can be organised through community service programmes, they may be similarly inexpensive, and foster community spirit and social commitment. Creative thinking and imagination is needed for new schemes at the local and national level.

An agenda for a sustainable economy

The Agenda that follows selects ten issues of strategic importance for movement towards a sustainable economy. They are also issues in which recent developments make significant progress politically feasible as well as environmentally essential. Such progress represents a minimum requirement for the five-year term of any government which wishes to be seen to take environmental sustainability seriously.

1. *Adjusting the National Accounts*
For many years, it has been apparent that the national accounts, and especially the computed National Income figure, overstate a country's annual production by failing to account for environmental depletion and degradation—both of which can be regarded in the terms of Figure 1 as the depreciation of natural capital—caused by the economic process. In 1993 the United Nations produced a Handbook on Integrated Environmental and Economic Accounting showing how calculations could be made in a set of environmental satellite accounts, in a manner consistent with the rest of the national accounts, so that the national product figures could be appropriately adjusted for environmental losses. As urged in a publication of the Club of Rome,[11] these recommendations now need to be implemented by national governments.

2. *Implementing Ecological Tax Reform*
In his 1994 budget, the UK Chancellor, Kenneth Clarke, accepted the principle of ecological tax reform (ETR), specifically stating: 'Taxes can play an important role in protecting the environment. . . . We propose that a new landfill tax should come into effect in 1996. . . . But I am determined

---

[11] W. Van Dieren, ed., *Taking Nature into Account*, Report to the Club of Rome, 1995.

© The Political Quarterly Publishing Co. Ltd. 1995.

not to impose additional costs on business overall. I shall therefore be looking at ways to offset the impact of the new tax by making further compensatory reductions in the level of employers' national insurance contributions—when the new tax is introduced. In brief, I want to raise tax on polluters to make further cuts in the tax on jobs' (p. 35). This needs to be the first stage of a general shift over ten to twenty years of the burden of taxation from labour, profits and general consumption to the use of environmental resources. As with the proposed landfill tax, this shift should be, and be seen to be, fiscally neutral, with the overall fiscal stance being set first on the basis of existing taxation patterns, and the mix of taxes then being changed so that ETR's objective of shifting the tax burden, rather than revenue-raising *per se*, is apparent.

3. *Harnessing Trade to Sustainable Development*
At the Marrakesh signing of the GATT Uruguay Round agreement, a Trade and Environment Committee of the new World Trade Organisation (WTO) was established as part of the Ministerial Declaration on Trade and Environment. The government needs to follow up hard on this opportunity to harness trade to sustainable development by ensuring that national environmental policymaking is not constrained by the thrust towards trade liberalisation.[12]

4. *Restructuring Transport*
The 1994 Report of the Royal Commission on Environmental Pollution made clear the extent of the present unsustainability of the UK's transport system in terms of meeting current and future transport needs with acceptable environmental consequences. Increases in road fuel duties are only part of the solution, and must be accompanied by major investments in public transport and comprehensive urban cycle routes, together with increasingly stringent restrictions on urban private car movements and on new developments that will generate traffic growth. Public awareness of the need for such measures is high, although their implementation will not be easy. To win support for a long-term strategy for a reduction in motoring mileage, determined measures that can yield early, widely perceived benefits through reductions in congestion and urban air pollution need to be adopted.

5. *Reforming Support for Agriculture*
The European Common Agricultural Policy (CAP) is one of the main global examples of subsidies that are environmentally destructive as well as economically inefficient. There is a case for subsidising farmers when they produce non-market environmental benefits as well as food. Subsidising them to farm in a way that damages the environment makes no sense at all. Recent CAP reforms have barely addressed this issue. Yet

---

[12] For a discussion of this issue, see P. Ekins, 'Harnessing Trade to Sustainable Development', paper presented at a seminar, Green College Centre, Green College, Oxford, 9 December 1994; and D. Esty, *Greening the GATT*, Institute for International Economics, Washington D.C, 1994.

51

© The Political Quarterly Publishing Co. Ltd. 1995.

such reform remains one of the main areas in which environmental and economic gains can be simultaneously achieved.

6. *Improving Energy Efficiency*

It is widely recognised that major gains in energy efficiency can be made at relatively low cost. However, there is no single or easy way to remove the informational, institutional and other obstacles to achieving these gains. Many proposals have been made in this area, including demand-side management, a government insulation programme, statutory labelling of energy-using appliances and buildings, and special incentives to overcome landlord-tenant problems. These need to be combined into a costed, single package of measures to bring the rates of increase of energy efficiency back to be levels achieved following the OPEC oil price rises of the 1970s.

7. *Forging a Green Industrial Strategy*

There is now much acceptance in industry of the need to move towards closed, low or no pollution industrial systems (see, for example, *Business International 1990*). What is needed at a governmental level are the incentives, cooperation and support to ensure that the development of such systems not only much reduces the impact of industry on the environment, but also provides a basis for innovation and competitiveness in the future. Many of the building blocks for such an industrial strategy now exist, such as the British Standard for Environmental Management, BS7750, the new emphasis on corporate environmental reporting,[13] the EC's voluntary regulation on eco-auditing, and numerous industry and environment groupings. By supporting the efforts of the corporate environmental pioneers in such areas as research and development, as well as applying both market-based and regulatory environmental instruments increasingly stringently, the government can help a green industrial strategy to emerge.

8. *Supporting Local Agenda 21 Initiatives*

Many local authorities are making impressive efforts to implement Agenda 21 locally. Government needs to give further encouragement and support to these efforts in such areas as recycling, planning powers and guidance, traffic management and provision of appropriate transport infrastructure, and publication of examples of best practice. A major Local Agenda 21 Conference convened by the government could inaugurate a new stage of national/local partnership for sustainability.

9. *Promoting Environmental Investment*

There are many areas in which investments are necessary to remedy past environmental damages or otherwise regenerate the environment. Woodlands, rivers, coastal bathing waters, wildlife habitats, and landscape features in national parks or other areas of natural beauty all warrant investment of some sort. Some could be forthcoming through a redirected

[13] See for example, DTTI (Deloitte Touche Tohmatsu International), London; ITSD (International Institute for Sustainable Development), Winnipeg; and Sustainability, London, *Coming Clean: Corporate Environmental Reporting*, 1993.

52

© The Political Quarterly Publishing Co. Ltd. 1995.

system of agricultural support. More could be channelled through the Local Agenda 21 initiatives of local authorities. More still could be effected through, for example, a new national scheme of Community Environmental Service. Government has a key role in identifying the opportunities and priorities, and establishing the methodologies of accounting and monitoring to ensure that such investment yields a good environmental return.

10. *Providing Cultural Leadership*

At root the crisis of environmental unsustainability is a crisis of values. We have not valued the environment enough—economically, socially or culturally. It is doubtful whether a society that thinks of itself as a 'consumer' society can develop the necessary habits and disciplines that are required to conserve the environment. Government can play an important role of cultural leadership in this respect through the themes it stresses, the images it chooses to project, the people and organisations it recognises and honours and the personal examples that it sets.

Conclusion

An environmentally sustainable economy cannot come about overnight, nor are its ultimate shape or characteristics clear. But there is no doubt at all about the first steps towards it that need to be taken, as outlined above, and enough is known of their implications for it to be certain that substantial moves towards sustainability are compatible with considerable material prosperity and a high quality of life. In fact, future standards of living are far more likely to be threatened by a failure to meet the challenge of sustainability than the reverse. The Worldwatch Institute has produced an annual *State of the World* report since 1984. In 1993 it concluded: 'The environmentally destructive activities of recent decades are now showing up in reduced productivity of croplands, forests, grasslands and fisheries; in the mounting of cleanup costs of toxic waste sites; in rising health care costs for cancer, birth defects, allergies, emphysema, asthma and other respiratory diseases; and in the spread of hunger'[14] (pp. 4–5). These trends mean: 'If we fail to convert our self-destructing economy into one that is environmentally sustainable, future generations will be overwhelmed by environmental degradation and social disintegration' (*ibid.*, p. 21).

The economic conversion to sustainability will not be easy, and will require hard choices, political courage and a long term view. But it offers easily the best prospect for the future health and well-being of people in the UK and elsewhere.

[14] L. R. Brown *et al.*, *State of the World 1993*, Earthscan, London, 1993.

53

© The Political Quarterly Publishing Co. Ltd. 1995.

© The Political Quarterly Publishing Co. Ltd. 1995. Published by Blackwell Publishers, 108 Cowley Road, Oxford OX4 1JF, UK and 238 Main Street, Cambridge, MA 02142, USA.

A GLOBAL LIVING WAGE

JAMES K. GALBRAITH*

An economic agenda for the Left?

I HAVE been in the agenda business a long time. My first effort, as a junior staffer aged 19, was published in 1971 as 'McGovern on the Issues' also known as 'The McGovern Encyclopedia' and was probably the historical origin of candidate agenda documents in U.S. presidential campaigns. Since then I have helped to prepare economic programmes for Morris Udall (1976), Jesse Jackson and Walter Mondale (1984), Gary Hart (1987) and Tom Harkin (1992): none successful. I also contributed chapters on monetary policy to agenda books published by the Democracy Project in 1988 and 1992, and provided in October of 1992 the original draft of the 'two-track' programme—short-run Keynesian stimulus with long-run deficit reduction—which formed the basis of President Clinton's soon-abandoned first-year economic programme.

Win or lose, left or centre-left candidates (in the U.S. anyway) really do need these agendas. They are expected. They reduce inconsistency and the number of things the candidates must memorise. They provide themes that an ultimate nominee can incorporate into a party platform, or that a losing candidate can press, to show that a lost campaign lives on.

One can doubt that the Left, in its present condition as an intellectual tendency or social force, needs any such agenda. If we had one, and it were coherent, we would disagree on its composition; whereas if it were incoherent (much more likely) it would do us more harm than good. At present we are in a state of division, compounded even more than usual by confusion. We must resolve our divisions before we can get down to the new agenda. And yet, as Keynes wrote in 1933, 'nothing is required, and nothing will avail, except a little clear thinking.'

Outflanked economic goals

So what are our goals? Revolution, class war and the dictatorship of the proletariat have slipped from fashion. So now, *full employment* is the hoariest phrase in our lexicon, the true mark of a Keynesian relic. Full employment was an objective well suited to a world of unionised industrial workers, a time when fewer women worked, when there were no migrants to speak of and little competition from Third World manufacturers. Today is very different: it is full of people who work, of overworked

* James K. Galbraith is Professor at the Lyndon B. Johnson School of Public Affairs and Department of Government, The University of Texas at Austin, and co-author of *Macroeconomics*, a text from Houghton-Mifflin.

people, of people who work desperately, all the time, in bad conditions, at the expense of their children and their social and cultural and political lives, and for whom work provides little relief from the desperation of their position. Full employment at high wages appears an impossibly remote objective to most people under these conditions, because it would mean not merely 'finding a job', but finding a job radically different from those known actually to exist. For this reason, full employment has largely lost its value as a political objective.

Economic growth has in any event supplanted full employment as the short-run policy objective of centre-left administrations. But it has the opposite problem: it is too easy. Growth *is* necessary, but it is not sufficient. Growth of what and for whom? Material shortages are not our problem. The same workers who compete for our jobs glut our markets with food, clothing and electronics, raising our real consumption wages, in effect, even as they undermine our employment security and wage structure.

Competitiveness and *Productivity* are the new entrants in this game. Alas! The first has become largely a cover for business policy goals in the fields of trade, technology and training, particularly for the goals (not always unworthy, though not specifically progressive in a political sense) of industries in the advanced sectors. The second is an economist's con trick. The profession has wasted twenty years' effort on the productivity problem without explaining the slowdown of productivity growth, and without advancing cures that go beyond ritual incantations to deficit reduction, savings, investment, education and infrastructure. These incantations form the basis of U.S. economic policy today. But having accepted the first step, deficit reduction, we find the others as remote as ever. Interest rates rose following deficit reduction in the U.S., private investment did not accelerate, and public investment simply disappeared from the agenda.

Recently, a bid for *sustainable development* has been heard. Loosely speaking, this means economic activity within the carrying capacity of the biosphere. The idea is appealing, but the science behind it remains under-developed. So far, we have seen clear applications only in a few sharply defined contexts, such as chlorofluorocarbons, tropical deforestation, and perhaps the bureaucratic culture of the World Bank. We are still far from being a green profession.

I wish I had a clear alternative to these slogans. What sort of society exactly do I want? Waiter! May I have the menu please? Ah yes, I'll take Luncheon Special #4, the Switzerland Club: decent, prosperous, peaceful, strong foundations, a mixed salad of public services on the side, a bit bland.

Sorry. There are obstacles, problems. The waiter is surly, you can't catch his eye. The cook is drunk, certain items aren't in the larder. And the price isn't listed. Are you sure you won't take the Thatcherburger with Cheese? That's what everyone else is having. That Thatcherburger focuses

© The Political Quarterly Publishing Co. Ltd. 1995.

the mind. What is it, exactly, that has gone wrong over the past twenty years, stripping our left agendas of force and our programmes of authenticity?

One answer is the huge increase in global manufactures trade with poor countries (much of it at the instigation of migrating multinational corporations), the pressures on employment and the wage structure of less-educated workers in the North, and the consequent sharp rise in inequality between the highly educated and the less so, manifested by falling wages in the US and by unemployment in Europe. We live in a world of intense wage pressure from an inexhaustible supply of cheap labour, foreign and domestic, although a wilful consensus among orthodox economists denies this. As a result, *we have an inequality crisis*.

We have also reached, or nearly so, the political limits of correcting this calamity through more progressive taxes, let alone welfare spending or employment programmes. Despite the association between education and earnings, we cannot hope to correct earnings inequality by equalising education. A higher minimum wage in the U.S. would be good; but how likely is it? Or, would Americans buy into a pro-domestic-union agenda, if they thought it meant increases in unemployment? More likely. And while defence of the poor is going to be high on all American Left programmes through the period of reactionary power in Congress, there is no chance that a broad political base can be built around this theme alone.

Our inequality crisis has a global origin. We may have to face the possibility that it only has a global solution, to be achieved, if at all, only in the very long term. Long-term programmes are difficult, but for a minority such as the Left, they have some political virtues. They transcend the electoral cycle. They will not be achieved in the short term, and therefore cannot be bought off or co-opted. And they can form the basis of a programme of education that may help develop political values for the generation to come, much as the Right inculcated 'small government', 'free enterprise', and 'individualism' during the long period from the New Deal to the Thatcher and Reagan Revolutions.

The need for a global approach

These days when the Left snarls, it is usually about something global. We saw this in the North American opposition to the NAFTA, the closest thing to a mobilisation of progressives on our continent in recent times. We saw it, I believe, in Danish, French and Norwegian opposition to Maastricht, in SPD opposition to a rapidly united Germany, and elsewhere. This reflects the reality many economists deny: competition with low-wage manufactures is depressing our wage structure and eliminating our low-skilled maufacturing jobs. (The position of British progressives with respect to European social policy and the actually higher level of continental real wages is, in this respect, the exception.)

© The Political Quarterly Publishing Co. Ltd. 1995.

A national approach is hard to resist. The Left has no transborder presence and its few levers of power are national in reach. Home constituencies can be mobilised, up to a point, against Japanese workers stealing our jobs, against Mexican workers stealing our jobs, against Chinese and Indians and Pakistanis and Turks and Arabs. But that is the problem. The national approach pits workers against workers, shades into matters of race and religion, and fosters drives for protection against the poor. It is also the approach that the Left's adversaries would have it take. When we do take it, *they* can portray *us* as the reactionaries, standing on invidious privilege and illegitimate doctrine. The national approach may be the maximum position, the strongest of the losers, because it makes for provisional alliances of progressives with the threatened and the scared: in the US Ralph Nader alongside the followers of Ross Perot. But if this ever were enough to win, it would be a formula for junior partnership in an ugly, repressive administration.

The global economy is a fact. Globalised business has the technological and competitive edge and will not give it up. Nations which export jet aircraft cannot take the national or protectionist view: the national position has been outflanked, and the day of autarchy (if it ever existed) will not come again.

Against this, a global approach has the virtue of both necessity and virtue itself. 'Global unionism' intoned a California AFL-CIO leader recently, 'is the only answer to global capitalism'. Global Keynesianism, one might very well add, is the only answer to global monetarism. But how can this be put into practice?

We must confront the global inequality crisis. For this, we must, in the final analysis, raise real wages in the countries with which our workers compete, expand their markets for our goods, and reduce their pressure on our wage structure. You cannot have this without free trade unions in those countries. You cannot have free trade unions in the long run without democracy (nor democracy without the freedom to form unions). You cannot have democracy without human rights. Our economic agenda should really begin a long way from economic policy itself, with the campaign for human rights, democracy, and free unionism around the world.

The liberation of South Africa is instructive. It was not decided by Sullivan codes, divestment, boycotts, embargoes and sanctions, although they helped. The liberation of Haiti (if it lasts) proceeded along similar lines, with a miraculous assist from United States soldiers. The present isolation of Burma must continue until the military tyrants there crack. The list could continue, but the point is already made. It is not the role of the North to raise real wages directly in the South, but it can be our role, as Northern progressives, to support those struggling for better conditions and to weaken those who stand in the way.

Revolutionary struggle is the exception. In South Korea and Taiwan, it is fair to say, progress towards democracy and human rights has come on

57

© The Political Quarterly Publishing Co. Ltd. 1995.

the back of prior social reform and a highly equal (and rapidly rising) real wage structure. This also happened in Japan years before. Something similar may begin to happen in China, which has the potential for either the best or the worst of outcomes. These countries are post-revolutionary in important respects. In most of the new industrial world, equalising revolutions never happened and are not in prospect. And so the advance of evolutionary democracy, and with its unionisation and the modernisation of both the state and the market, must accompany industrial growth. This must be our way towards a more equal and more stable world, if we are not to face an unending stream of pressures to average down.

One tentative agenda has multiple elements aimed at this single critical point. It has, however, only one element traditionally recognised as economic, put here in the first position.

1. Secure low and stable interest rates by whatever means. High interest is the great un-equaliser in a debt-dependent world. When the Federal Reserve or the Bundesbank tightens, every capital market in the world slumps. Those which are most important for the development process fall fastest and most. Debtors suffer, including national debtors, while creditors gain. The currencies of the advanced countries rise, while those of the poor countries fall; this reduces real wages in poor countries and intensifies pressure on advanced-country wages. Advanced exports, which support the development process, fall as Third World purchasing power and the capacity to finance declines.

Of all the unexploited opportunities of the Left, monetary policy is surely the most central. It has universal impact, and for this reason a programme focused on low interest rates should have very broad appeal. Moreover, global monetary policy remains under the control of the advanced powers, and therefore within the ambit of our political systems. Central banks are vulnerable to politics in ways that much else on a Left agenda is not.

2. Cut arms budgets and the arms trade. We cannot stop world conflict in this way; but we can work to reduce levels of violence and the power of repressive states, as well as the threats which provide increasingly thin justification for continued military excess in our home countries. The arms trade is a visible cancer, a major source of corruption, and it is linked to the wage competition faced by Northern workers. The cynical and self-serving view that nothing can or should be done about this is an economic fallacy, as well as a human outrage.

3. Support human rights campaigns, but especially in countries where economic relations are closest and leverage is best. Human rights has multiple dimensions. It surely includes the personal political freedoms. It should include recognition of union rights, a free and flexible job market and a social safety net. The capacity to organise one's own farm or enterprise, and to finance it, alongside the right to quit and not starve, are important social safeguards and upward forces on real wages. At the same time, human rights campaigns need to be subjected to a reality-check.

© The Political Quarterly Publishing Co. Ltd. 1995.

Tactics that make sense in Haiti or Guatemala or even South Africa may be unworkable when applied to China.

4. As a particular priority in an increasingly ugly political environment, the Left should support full labour rights for *migrant* workers. The drive to punish migrants deflects attention from a crucial question: why do employers hire illegal migrants in the first place? The answer in the United States is that they can pay them less, or provide working conditions that domestic workers generally would not tolerate. If, in the United States, we could curb the fear of deportation and reestablish union power, the wages and conditions for illegal migrants would *per force* rise to domestic standards. Then, the problem would resolve itself: the number of migrants would necessarily decline, for employment would be driven mainly by genuine shortages of legal workers (as in Europe), and there would be no incentive to use migrants instead of nationals to undermine domestic labour standards.

5. Support environmental campaigns. The destruction of environments is virtually never a positive development force. Rather it usually comes at the expense of urban investments that are desperately needed, and works for the benefit of the rich, not the poor. We should by all means accept the exported products of urban Brazil, and finance the infrastructure of Sao Paulo. We should forego, and even ban if necessary, the import of tropical hardwoods, just as we do exotic birds, rhinoceros horns and the skins of endangered species. No poor people are getting rich off rapacious extraction of the world's remaining bio-reserves.

6. Begin an organised campaign to reorganise or even replace the IMF and World Bank with organisations whose priorities are democratic development, human rights and environmental protection, not debt repayment and free markets to no discernible higher purpose. The failures of both agencies are so rampant in recent years, even highly reputable mainstreamers are disaffected. This opportunity should not be missed. Nor should new agencies, such as the nascent World Trade Organisation, be exempted from scrutiny as they develop.

There are certain to be many more important measures omitted here; but I think my agenda is clear. The Left should stop recycling Keynesian employment policies, New Deal public works and welfare programmes and the Civil Rights movements. As social forces these are spent, in some cases corrupted, and as economic programmes they have been outflanked. In the U.S. the fate of Clinton's health proposals is poignant proof: it was not the political issue he hoped for, and even if it had been, it was clearly the last such 'New Deal' issue.

The Left in the US have been losing in part because we are viewed, rightly, as the guardians of 'old ideas'. As such, we have lost our moral standing, our voice. Our critique no longer penetrates very far, nor seems terribly relevant. We have said little about the inequality crisis, and what we have said generally focuses on the very rich, the truly poor, and the unemployed. We are mobilised to the worthy defence of food and housing

59

© The Political Quarterly Publishing Co. Ltd. 1995.

programmes, but we have had little to offer the employed worker. For these reasons, we have been bypassed on the Right by the neo-liberal advocates of 'education, training infrastructure and R&D', alongside 'welfare reform', migration 'reform' and get-tough-on-crime.

At the same time, we have separated ourselves, as progressive economists, from progressive friends who campaign for human rights, democracy, disarmament and the environment. This distances those on the Left who are not economists from those who are, and leaves the Left itself without a coherent progressive economics. As economists and progressives, we are neglecting our duties to our friends. Our silence on these issues undermines their work, which has been in most respects more important recently than our own.

In conclusion, in our global economy, peace, human rights, democracy, free unionism and the environment, alongside low and stable interest rates, are and must be shown to be the background of Left economic policy itself. This is not hard for the larger public to understand. By redefining ourselves around these issues, we may yet give a coherent identity and programme to the Left, and set the stage for a long campaign to achieve a global living wage.

© The Political Quarterly Publishing Co. Ltd. 1995.

© The Political Quarterly Publishing Co. Ltd. 1995. Published by Blackwell Publishers, 108 Cowley Road, Oxford OX4 1JF, UK and 238 Main Street, Cambridge, MA 02142, USA.

EMPLOYMENT IN THE UNITED KINGDOM: TRENDS AND PROSPECTS

KEN COUTTS AND BOB ROWTHORN*

PAID employment plays a central part in modern life. It is the main source of income for most adults. It provides a context for social interaction and cooperation with others and for many it is a rewarding experience in itself. It shapes the lives of almost everyone and provides the structure around which the wider society is built. As the activities of millions of housewives and others testify, paid employment is not the only kind of useful work, but in the modern world it is normally the matrix within which other forms of work are organised. The primacy of paid employment has been rightly questioned by many feminists, who argue for a more balanced relationship between family and work, and for a new division of labour between men and women. Significant changes have already occurred in this domain and there will be more in the future. However, whilst its role may alter, paid employment will continue to be of central importance in our society.

In this chapter, we describe the present employment situation in the UK and consider future prospects. We show how the nature of employment has become increasingly diverse in recent years with the spread of part-time and self-employment and the large scale entry of married women into the labour market. It has also been characterised by increasing inequality in the form of greater unemployment and insecurity for some, together with a much wider dispersion of earnings. We discuss how far these trends are likely to continue in the future and what can be done about their more harmful aspects. The basic problem is a general shortage of demand for labour in the British economy, which impoverishes millions of people and creates insecurity for millions of others. We argue that this situation is not inevitable. On the contrary, the demand for labour is now rising and the prospects for sustaining the present economic recovery are good. If this recovery can be sustained, then unemployment should fall significantly over the next decade. We conclude the chapter by suggesting how to bring down unemployment still further.

* Ken Coutts is a Lecturer and Bob Rowthorn is Professor of Economics in the Faculty of Economics and Politics, University of Cambridge. The authors wish to thank John Wells for helpful comments on the text, but any remaining errors are the responsibility of the authors alone. We also thank Bill Wells of the Department of Employment for useful discussion on some of the issues raised in the first section of the article.

61

Diversity and inequality

The British labour market is one of the most diverse in the OECD. Much of this diversity reflects personal choice, but much is the undesired outcome of factors beyond individual control and is therefore a symptom of inequality.

The extent of diversity can be gauged from the following overview of the labour market:[1]

- Some 15.7 million people (62 per cent of all UK workers) were full-time, permanent employees in Spring 1993. In addition there were 9.7 million engaged in 'non-standard' employment as part-time, temporary, self-employed or unpaid family workers or on a Government training scheme.
- In Spring 1994, full-time employees accounted for 73.4 per cent of total weekly hours performed in the British Economy. The remaining hours were divided almost equally between the full-time self-employed (14.3 per cent) and part-timers (12.3 per cent).
- The number of people in non-standard employment has increased by 1.25 million since 1986. The proportion of men in such employment has risen from 18 per cent in 1981 to 27 per cent in 1993, whereas amongst women it has remained roughly constant at about 50 per cent.
- The increase in non-standard working amongst men is due to the expansion of self-employment, which rose strongly in the 1980s, but has stabilised in recent years at around 17 per cent of male employment.
- The share of employees in temporary work is around 6 per cent. This figure has remained roughly constant over the past decade.
- 92 per cent of employees, over 29 years old, work for the same employer as they did one year before.[2]
- 96 per cent of full-time employees and 88 per cent of part-time employees work in 'permanent' jobs (Table 1).
- The average duration of part-time jobs is half that of full-time jobs.[3] This difference may be partly due to a higher rate of voluntary quits amongst part-timers.
- The pattern of non-standard working is very varied and there are major differences between men and women. Three quarters of the

[1] This summary draws heavily on two articles by Gary Watson: 'Hours of Work in Great Britain and Europe', *Employment Gazette*, November 1992, and 'The Flexible Workforce and Patterns of Working Hours in the UK', *Employment Gazette*, July 1994. All data refer to Spring 1993 unless otherwise stated.
[2] The figure given here refers to all persons in a job one week before the Spring 1991 Labour Force Survey was conducted and also in a job one year previously.
[3] Paul Gregg and Jonathan Wadsworth, 'Job Tenure and Job Security in the 1980s', *Oxford Review of Economic Policy*, Spring 1995.

© The Political Quarterly Publishing Co. Ltd. 1995.

TABLE 1   EMPLOYMENT STATUS BY SEX: UNITED KINGDOM, SPRING 1993

	All		Men		Women	
	(000s)	(per cent)	(000s)	(per cent)	(000s)	(per cent)
Permanent Employees						
Full-time	15,685	61.8	10,204	73.2	5,480	47.9
Part-time	4,718	18.6	513	3.7	4,204	36.7
Temporary Employees						
Full-time	659	2.6	393	2.8	266	2.3
Part-time	624	2.5	174	0.2	451	3.9
Self-Employed						
Full-time	2,590	10.2	2,171	15.6	419	3.7
Part-time	589	2.3	199	1.4	390	3.4
Other						
Government training schemes	359	1.4	236	1.7	123	1.1
Unpaid family workers	154	0.6	43	1.0	111	1.0
All in employment	25,381	100	13,934	100	11,446	100

Source: Employment Gazette, July 1994, Table 2.

63

© The Political Quarterly Publishing Co. Ltd. 1995.

self-employed are men, whereas 85 per cent of part-timers and 56 per cent of temporary employees are women.

- 18 per cent of employees (3.9 million) usually or occasionally work shifts.
- 12 per cent of employees (2.6 million) work 'flexitime'—10 per cent of men and 14 per cent of women.
- In 1990, 9.7 per cent of UK employees usually worked fewer than 16 hours per week in their main job compared to a European Union average of 5 per cent; 16 per cent of UK employees usually worked over 48 hours per week compared to an EU average of 6.8 per cent.
- In 1991, average hours were 17 per week for part-time employees, 43.6 for full-time employees, and 53.5 per week for the full-time self-employed.
- 89 per cent of women and 72 per cent of men working part-time do not want a full-time job.[4]
- 6 million women and 3 million men in the age range 16–64 years are officially classified as economically inactive. The number has been rising for men but falling for women.
- In Spring 1994 women held 45 per cent of all jobs and performed 35.4 per cent of all hours of paid work in Great Britain.

Inequality

Inequality in the British labour market has a number of dimensions. A majority of the labour force enjoys secure, reasonably paid employment in jobs with broadly acceptable hours of work and conditions of employment. In this group are most full-time employees, together with many part-timers and the self-employed. However, there is a substantial minority who do not enjoy these advantages. Earnings dispersion has increased dramatically under Conservative governments since 1979 and there is now a large army of the 'working poor', whose wages are insufficient to keep them above the poverty line.[5] The number of people in precarious employment has grown. The boom and bust character of the economy has made many 'permanent' jobs insecure and led some employers to take on part-timers because they are easier to sack then full-timers. There are now millions of unemployed people, many of whom do not appear in the official unemployment statistics but are classified as 'economically inactive'. A novel feature of the present situation is the increased incidence of two-earner and no-earner families. In the former, both men and women have paid employment and their financial situation is relatively prosperous. In the latter, there is either a lone parent who is not working, or a couple without stable employment for either partner—either

---

[4] *The Labour Force Survey*, Winter 1993/94.
[5] For evidence on trends in earnings inequality in the UK and other OECD countries see Paul Gregg and Stephen Machin, 'Is the UK rise in inequality different?' in Ray Barrell, ed., *The UK Labour Market*, Cambridge University Press, Cambridge, 1994.

© The Political Quarterly Publishing Co. Ltd. 1995.

way the result is normally chronic poverty. This division between job-rich and job-poor households is perhaps the most serious inequality in our society. Gregg and Wadsworth (1995) document the development of inequality. They show that there is now a large pool of people of working age who live in a state of chronic insecurity and poverty. In addition to the long-term unemployed, this pool consists of millions of people who switch frequently into and out of employment, moving from one badly paid, part-time job to the next with spells of unemployment in between. Many of them have little chance of obtaining the secure or full-time employment they desire.

Table 2 presents some calculations we have made to indicate the extent of inequality in the British labour market. The assumptions underlying this table are crude and the numbers shown are really just informed guesses. Even so, the orders of magnitude are probably right.

According to the Spring 1994 Labour Force Survey, there are 27.6 million people in the labour force in Great Britain. In addition there is an unknown number of people who might be willing to work if a reasonable job were available. Some of these are recorded in the Survey as 'discouraged workers' who have given up looking for a job as hopeless.[6] Others are recorded as permanently sick, disabled or retired. There are many who say that they do not want a job, but would probably change their minds if jobs were plentiful. According to the Winter 1993/1994 Labour Force Survey, there were 1,035 million economically inactive persons who were available for work and would like a job, but were not actively seeking a job.[7] We include all of these amongst the hidden unemployed. In addition, there were 1,339 million persons who would like a job but were not available for work in the next two weeks because of sickness, family responsibilities or some other reason. We include one-third of these amongst the hidden unemployed. This gives a total of approximately 1.5 million, of which 0.6 million are men and 0.9 million are women.

When hidden unemployment is taken into account, we get a revised figure of 29.1 million for the British labour force. This is divided in our table into three main categories: primary, intermediate and disadvantaged, of which the latter is subdivided into employed and unemployed. The heading 'primary' covers only full-time employees with secure, reasonably paid jobs. We assume that 80 per cent of full-time workers belong in this category, whilst the remaining 20 per cent are classified as disadvantaged because of low pay and/or insecurity. The heading 'intermediate' covers

---

[6] The Spring 1984 Labour Force Survey classified about 2.5 million as 'marginally active' at a time when about 2.9 million were unemployed. See the *Employment Gazette, op. cit.,* January 1986. Estimates of the 'disappearing men' made by John Wells suggest that between 1979 and 1993 over 1 million became inactive, partly because of more tertiary education and voluntary early retirement, but mainly because of the lack of job opportunities. John Wells, 'The Missing Million', *Employment Labour Forum,* 1994.

[7] *Employment Gazette,* Table 4, page LFS4, July 1994.

© The Political Quarterly Publishing Co. Ltd. 1995.

TABLE 2   THE TWO-THIRDS/ONE-THIRD LABOUR FORCE: GREAT BRITAIN, SPRING 1994 (millions)

	Full-time Employees	Part-time Employees	Self-employed	Government Programmes & unpaid family	ILO Unemployed	Economically inactive	All millions	All (Per cent)
Primary	13.5	0.0	0.0	0.0	0.0	0.0	13.5	(46)
Intermediate	0.0	4.1	2.4	0.1	0.0	0.0	6.6	(23)
Disadvantaged:								
employed	2.4	1.4	0.8	0.4	0.0	0.0	4.9	(17)
unemployed*	0.0	0.0	0.0	0.0	2.6	1.5	4.1	(14)
All	15.9	5.4	3.2	0.5	2.6	1.5	29.1	(100)

Source: Labour Force Survey.
* Includes hidden unemployment amongst the economically inactive.

© The Political Quarterly Publishing Co. Ltd. 1995.

employed persons who are not full-time employees, but have acceptable jobs in terms of pay and security. We assume that 70 per cent of part-timers and the self-employed fall into this category, while the remaining 30 per cent are disadvantaged. There is also a small number of unpaid family workers and persons on government training schemes who are allocated between the intermediate and disadvantaged categories as shown in the table. Finally, anyone who is unemployed is classified as disadvantaged. This includes the hidden unemployed amongst the economically inactive population.

On the basis of these assumptions, we calculate that 13.5 million of the labour force are in the primary sector, and another 6.6 million in the intermediate sector. This gives a total of 20.1 million whose jobs are broadly satisfactory in terms of security and pay. There is considerable diversity within this group with regard to hours of work and employment status, but these differences reflect in large measure the preferences of those concerned. The final category consists of the disadvantaged, of whom there are an estimated 9 million, of which 4.9 million are employed and 4.1 million unemployed. Despite their very approximate nature, these figures reveal clearly the existence of what has been called the 'two-thirds/one-third' society in Britain. 70 per cent of the labour force are financially comfortable and reasonably secure, while 30 per cent live in either insecurity or comparative poverty.

Future trends

There has been a significant increase in non-standard jobs in the UK in recent decades. Many politicians and journalists claim that this trend will continue indefinitely and that permanent, full-time jobs will become a thing of the past. 'People must accept change', we are told, and can no longer 'expect a job for life'. Before evaluating such claims, we must make an important distinction. A 'permanent' job is not the same as a job for life. Most jobs today are permanent in the sense that the employees concerned can reasonably expect to continue in them and have some degree of legal or institutional job protection. If the employees concerned do their work properly and their employer prospers, they can expect to keep their job. If their firm does badly or restructures its operations, or they neglect their work, then even 'permanent' employees may lose their jobs. Moreover, many permanent workers leave their jobs voluntarily, especially when they are young. Thus, although most workers are permanent employees, relatively few have a 'job for life'. But there is nothing new about this. The proportion of the labour force remaining with a single employer for their whole working lives has always been small, and it has been quite normal for people to occupy several jobs in the course of a lifetime. Apart from a comparatively small minority, mainly in the public sector, few people have ever enjoyed an open-ended job guarantee.

© The Political Quarterly Publishing Co. Ltd. 1995.

The real issue today is not whether people can expect a job for life, but what kind of job security they enjoy and what are the prospects for re-employment if they lose their jobs? These depend partly on government labour market policy, but above all on the general performance of the economy. If the present economic recovery can be sustained and the booms and slumps of the past 20 years avoided, the kind of job security which most workers enjoyed in the 1950s and 1960s can be restored. Fewer people will lose their jobs, and those who do so will find another job with relative ease just as they did before. On the other hand, if the economic instability of the past 20 years is repeated, the number of people in insecure forms of employment may continue to rise.

After this preamble, let us now consider the three main forms of non-standard jobs: self-employment, part-time employment and temporary employment.

TABLE 3   SELF-EMPLOYMENT AND PART-TIME
EMPLOYMENT IN SEVEN OECD COUNTRIES (per cent
of total employment)

	1979	1983	1990
	Self-employment*		
Canada	6.7	7.1	7.2
France	10.6	10.5	10.5
Germany	7.7	–	8.4
Italy	18.9	20.7	22.4
Japan	14.0	13.3	12.0
United Kingdom	**6.6**	**8.6**	**11.5**
United States	7.1	7.7	7.5
	Part-time employment		
Canada	12.5	15.4	15.4
France	8.2	9.7	12.0
Germany	11.4	12.6	13.2
Italy	5.3	4.6	5.7
Japan	15.4	16.2	17.6
United Kingdom	**16.4**	**19.4**	**21.8**
United States	16.4	18.4	16.9

Source: OECD Employment Outlook, July 1991, Tables 2.9 and 2.12.
* Non-agricultural, excluding unpaid family workers.

Self-employment

In the heyday of Thatcherism it was often said that self-employment is the wave of the future and that ever more people will choose to work for themselves. The evidence does not support this view. As can be seen from

© The Political Quarterly Publishing Co. Ltd. 1995.

Table 3, British experience with regard to self-employment in the 1980s was unusual by international standards. No other OECD country experienced the explosive growth in self-employment that occurred in Britain during the 1980s, and in many of them the share of self-employment was either stable or fell. As a result, the share of workers who are self-employed in Britain is now amongst the highest in the OECD.

TABLE 4   SELF-EMPLOYMENT BY INDUSTRY: GREAT BRITAIN, SPRING 1984–94 (per cent of total employment)

	1984	1990	1994
Agriculture and fishing	48	52	54
Manufacturing*	4	6	6
Construction	30	40	44
Distribution, Hotels and Restaurants	17	16	14
Transport	9	11	11
Banking, Finance and Insurance, etc.	12	15	15
Other Services†	6	8	8
All industries	**11**	**13**	**13**

Source: Labour Force Survey.
* Includes energy and water.
† Includes public administration etc.

The British experience during the 1980s was so unusual that it was singled out for special examination in a recent survey of self-employment by the *OECD Employment Outlook*.[8] After considering various explanations, the survey concluded that the rapid growth of self-employment in the UK during this period was 'somewhat puzzling', but in their view the main factor was the particularly vigorous government policy action to promote such employment. Table 4 shows what has happened to self-employment in particular industries over the past decade. During the 1980s the share of self-employment rose in every single industry with the exception of distribution, where there was a slight fall, presumably reflecting the decline of small shops in the face of competition from large supermarkets. Since 1990, there has been a modest increase in the share of self-employment in the construction industry. There has also been a continuing rise in the share of self-employment in agriculture, caused by the impact of mechanisation on the demand for wage labour. However, employment in agriculture is now so small that this is of minor importance. Meanwhile, the decline of self-employment in distribution has accelerated. Apart from these changes, the share of self-employment seems to

[8] *OECD Employment Outlook*, July 1992, chapter 4.

69

© The Political Quarterly Publishing Co. Ltd. 1995.

KEN COUTTS AND BOB ROWTHORN

have stabilised across most of the economy. The much-heralded shift towards self-employment of the 1980s has apparently come to an end. This is not surprising, given that its share is now so high by international standards and that practical experience has made clear some of the pitfalls of this type of employment.

Part-time employment

As can be seen from Table 3, Britain has the largest share of people working part-time of any large OECD country. Moreover, apart from France, it is the only large country to have experienced a major increase in this share during the 1980s. The United States is often seen as the model towards which the British labour market is converging, but in fact part-time working is both less common in the U.S. than here and has actually fallen in recent years. These comparisons suggest that the growth of part-time working in Britain may slow down in the not too distant future and its share of total employment may stabilise or even begin to fall.

What happens to the share of part-time working depends on how many full-time jobs are created in the future. Full-time employment is highly sensitive to the economic cycle. When times are good the number of full-time jobs increases rapidly, and when times are bad the opposite happens. During the economic recovery of 1984–90, the number of people in full-time employment rose by 1.8 million, of which 1.1 million were employees and the rest self-employed. Moreover, the proportion of married women working full-time increased strongly during this period, from 45 per cent in 1984 to 50 per cent in 1990. In the recession which followed, many of these full-time jobs were lost; but if the present economic recovery could be sustained for some years, the result would be a renewed supply of full-time employment. Some of these jobs would be filled by men and women who would otherwise work part-time, and others by the unemployed or people currently outside of the labour force altogether. Either way, the rising trend of part-time employment would be slowed down and might even be reversed.

Another factor to consider is the changing educational level of women. Most women with children now work outside the home. However, there is a strong correlation between their level of education and the extent to which they work full-time. For example, amongst women with the youngest child under the age of five, only 2 per cent of unskilled manual workers work full-time as compared to 34 per cent of professional and managerial workers.[9] Amongst women with the youngest child aged ten or over, the figures are 5 per cent and 63 per cent respectively. This is hardly surprising, since highly qualified women earn far more than unskilled women and they can afford to pay for the additional childcare and other costs involved in full-time working. They also have well-defined career

[9] *Social Trends*, 1993 Edition, Table 4.8.

70

© The Political Quarterly Publishing Co. Ltd. 1995.

paths and lose more if they stop working or work only part-time. As women become better qualified and move up the occupational hierarchy, it is likely that the number of mothers desiring full-time work will increase quite rapidly.

Temporary employment

The share of temporary employment in the UK is one of the lowest in the EU. In 1991 some 5.3 per cent of UK employees worked in temporary jobs compared with an EU average of 10.1 per cent. Moreover, the UK figure shows no sign of increasing. In certain continental countries, especially France and Spain, fixed term contracts have been increasingly used as a way of evading the extensive legal protection which full-time employees enjoy. In the UK, the regulatory regime is relatively liberal and permanent employees receive less legal protection. Employers thus have less incentive to circumvent the law by using temporary employment contracts. Unless the regulatory regime in the UK is drastically altered, there is no reason to expect a major growth in temporary employment.

Conclusion

The evidence does not support the claim that permanent, full-time employment is becoming a thing of the past. On the contrary, the shift towards self-employment may already have come to an end, the growth of part-time employment is likely to slow down in the medium term, whilst temporary employment is not increasing.

In the following section, we argue that the demand for labour is likely to recover significantly over the next decade in the UK, and that even more employment could be created given appropriate policy measures. If this happens, many of the new jobs will be full-time and the relative importance of both part-time and self-employment may eventually decline. Even if the economic recovery is weak, there will still be a very large number of people in full-time employment. Either way, this will raise the question of what is meant by a full-time job. As more women enter the labour force and more of them work full-time, there is a growing debate about the relationship between work and family life. There is pressure to organise paid work in ways more compatible with domestic responsibilities and with modern views on the sexual division of labour. Alongside the traditional demand for more professional child-care, there is an increasing emphasis on shorter and more flexible hours for male and female full-timers alike. This important issue is not considered in the present chapter, although there is a brief reference to the impact of shorter hours in the following discussion of employment creation.[10]

[10] For a thorough discussion of this issue see Patricia Hewitt, *About Time: the Revolution in Work and Family Life*, IPPR, London, 1993.

71

© The Political Quarterly Publishing Co. Ltd. 1995.

Towards full employment

Official projections suggest that the British labour force will grow by 1.4 million between 1994 and 2005. Of this increase, 0.9 million is due to population growth and 0.5 million is associated with the entry of more women into the labour market.[11] Given that officially-measured unemployment is currently 2.6 million, it would require the creation of at least 4.0 million extra jobs to achieve full employment by 2005. This calculation ignores any hidden unemployment which may still exist. It also ignores the fact that some of the hidden unemployed may become economically active given the increase demand for labour we envisage. The arithmetic is shown in the first part of Table 5. To explore the feasibility of achieving this target, we begin by presenting some projections based on a simple econometric model of the UK economy.[12] The main purpose of this model is to examine how fast the economy can grow, and how many jobs can be created, within the constraints arising from the need to remain internationally solvent. If the balance of payments is strong, rapid economic growth and a high rate of job creation is feasible. Conversely, if the balance of payments is weak, growth will be slow and job creation more difficult.

TABLE 5   HOW MANY JOBS
REQUIRED? (millions)

Labour force growth 1994–2005		1.4
population growth	0.9	
activity rate	0.5	
Unemployment 1994		2.6
Extra jobs required by 2005		4.0

Following the country's exit from the ERM in 1992, the trade performance of UK manufacturing has improved markedly. Exports have risen strongly, helped by the low pound and also a recovery in world trade. Oil production and property income from overseas have risen, whilst the City of London remains a major export earner. As a result, the overall balance of payments is now stronger than it was a few years ago, although there is still a small deficit. Using our model, we ask the following question.

[11] The figure of 0.5 million reflects the combined influence of increased female participation (0.7 million) and reduced male participation (0.2 million) mainly due to more young men in education.
[12] The model derives originally from the work of Wynne Godley and his colleagues in the Cambridge Economic Policy Group, although it has been modified to provide a more detailed analysis of foreign trade and payments. This model was developed under the aegis of the Cambridge-Harvard Research Project, and work on it is now continuing within the ESRC Centre for Business Research, University of Cambridge.

72

© The Political Quarterly Publishing Co. Ltd. 1995.

How fast can the economy grow over the next decade without making this deficit much worse? The answer is given by a conditional forecast which we call the Base Projection. This projection does not tell us what will actually happen, but what is feasible given the country's predicted balance of payments performance, assuming no major shocks or changes in government policy.

Figures 1(a) and 1(b) show what happens to output and the balance of payments under the Base Projection. After recovering quite fast from the 1990–93 recession, the growth rate of GDP settles down to about 2.1 per cent. At this growth rate, the balance of payments deficit remains small and Britain remains solvent. With significantly faster growth, imports would surge ahead, the deficit would explode and the country's foreign debt would mushroom.

The behaviour of employment under the Base Projection is shown in Figure 1(c). There is a sustained increase in employment over the entire period of the projection, and by 2005 an extra 1.9 million jobs are created. However, for reasons explained above, the number of people seeking work is also greater, so the fall in unemployment is modest (Figure 2). By 2005 there are still 2.1 million unemployed, which is 7.4 per cent of the labour force.

Narrowing the gap

Despite a significant rise in employment under the Base Projection, the level of unemployment remains unacceptably high. What might be done to improve this performance?

Measures for cutting unemployment can be divided into two groups: those which reduce the number of people seeking jobs and those which increase the number of jobs available. As an illustration, we present the following package of measures that operates in both directions at once.

• *Education*. Compared to other countries at a similar level of economic development, Britain has a very low proportion of young men and women staying on at school and higher education. This both inflates the labour force and inhibits our economic performance. Official projections foresee some growth in the proportion of the population in full-time education, but even by 2005 this proportion will be well below the levels currently observed in certain other countries. If Britain were to follow the examples of South Korea, an extra 1 million British males aged 16 to 24 years would be in full-time education in addition to the increase already envisaged in official projections. With Singaporean levels of education, an extra 600,000 people in the age group 16 to 19 years would be in full-time education.[13]

[13] These estimates are derived from figures on economic activity given in the *ILO Yearbook of Labour Statistics 1993*, and the *Employment Gazette*, April 1994. In South Korea in 1992 economic activity rates for males in the age groups 15–19 years and 20–24 years were

73

© The Political Quarterly Publishing Co. Ltd. 1995.

There is clearly massive scope for expending education in Britain, but to achieve the level of Korea or Singapore by 2005 might be an unrealistic goal. Instead, we assume the more realistic, but still ambitious objective of 300,000 extra people in full-time education.

- *Public Services.* There are many areas where a modest expansion of public services would be both desirable and popular. More teachers and other staff would be required for the educational programme outlined above. More workers would be an invaluable aid to relieve the overstretched local community services for the aged and the infirm. More workers could usefully be employed in the health service. The list is long and familiar. Such an expansion in public services would cost money, but the cost would be relatively small since there would be an offsetting fall in unemployment and related social security benefits. The government would also claw back part of the cost, since the extra workers would pay taxes. Even so, there would be some extra costs and the money would have to be found somehow.[14] We assume that employment in the public services is raised by 250,000. This represents an increase of 6 per cent over the 1993 level. However, since private sector employment is also increasing, the share of public services in total employment would not rise.

- *Output.* There is a variety of measures which might improve the competitive performance of the economy and its ability to raise output. One is the expansion of education described above, although most of the benefits would be felt beyond the time period we are concerned with. Another might be a system of investment incentives to encourage capacity creation in manufacturing and internationally traded services. Again, the list is long and familiar. We assume that such measures raise the rate of output growth over the period 1993–2003 by 0.1 per cent per annum. This very small increase is assumed to occur entirely in the private sector and is in addition to the expansion of public services mentioned above. With given labour productivity, the result is an extra 250,000 jobs by 2005.

- *Hours of Work.* In line with the campaign for 'family friendly' employment policies, we assume that the hours worked by the average worker

---

14.4 and 62.3 per cent respectively. For the UK in 2005 the official projections are 55.8 per cent (16–19 years) and 77.8 per cent. In the case of Singapore, for the age group 15–19 years economic activity rates were 30 per cent for males and 28.6 per cent for females. Projected figures for the age group 16–19 years in the UK for 2005 are 55.8 per cent for men and 59.3 per cent for women. Differences between activity rates in the UK and other countries are assumed to reflect different levels of educational participation (adjusting for the fact that UK figures for the younger age group refer to 16–19 years, whilst those of other countries refer to 15–19 years).

[14] For an extended discussion on the role of public services in employment creation, see Andrew Glyn and Bob Rowthorn, 'European Unemployment Policies', in Jonathan Michie and John Grieve Smith, eds., *Unemployment in Europe*, Academic Press, London, 1994.

© The Political Quarterly Publishing Co. Ltd. 1995.

decline by 0.3 per cent per year. By 2005 this implies a cumulative reduction of 1 hour per week. We assume that two-thirds of this reduction is offset by greater effort or a more efficient use of labour. As a result, the impact on employment is only 0.1 per cent a year. Even so, this generates an additional 250,000 jobs by the end of the period.

The effect of these measure can be summarised as follows:

* education—300,000 cut in labour force
* public services—250,000 extra jobs
* output growth–250,000 extra jobs
* hours of work—250,000 extra jobs

Individually these changes are small, but their combined effect is substantial. Figure 3 shows what happens when they are superimposed on our Base Projection. By 2005 unemployment falls to 1.1 million or 3.8 per cent of the labour force. The caveat is that a sustained growth in job opportunities would itself encourage many economically inactive workers to look for work. Nonetheless, it shows that unemployment could be brought down to levels not seen in Britain since the mid-1970s. This may not be full employment, but it is not far off.

Conclusions

This chapter has shown how the labour market in Britain is characterised by both diversity and inequality. Much of this diversity is a reflection of the preferences of the labour force and will continue to be a major feature of the economy in future. Indeed, for full-time workers there will be increasing pressure for greater flexibility of hours and conditions of work. On the other hand, some of the major trends towards diversity, such as the spread of part-time and self-employment, are likely to slow down. This will be most probable if the present economic recovery can be sustained, since full-time jobs will then be created in large numbers. Following Britain's departure from the ERM, the prospects for a sustained recovery are now good. Through a combination of intelligent macroeconomic policies to keep the recovery going and the kind of special measures outlined in this article, it should be possible to bring unemployment down to a million or so within a decade. This would end the poverty of many who would otherwise by unemployed, and would help many others in employment who are condemned to low pay and insecurity by the lack of demand for labour. It would thereby contribute to the revitalisation of the community, which is the theme of this book.

© The Political Quarterly Publishing Co. Ltd. 1995.

FIGURE 1   Base Projection

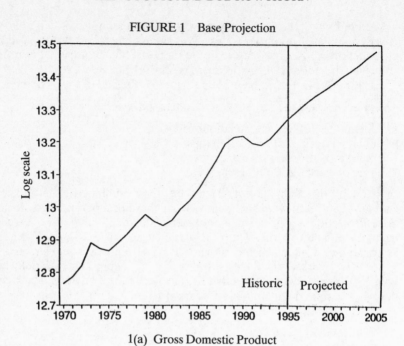

1(a) Gross Domestic Product

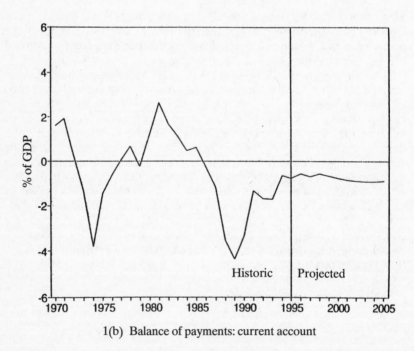

1(b) Balance of payments: current account

76

© The Political Quarterly Publishing Co. Ltd. 1995.

EMPLOYMENT IN THE UK

FIGURE 1   Base Projection (cont'd)

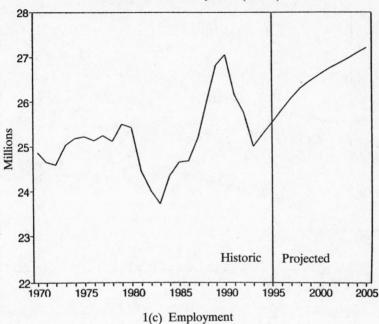

1(c) Employment

FIGURE 2   Base Projection

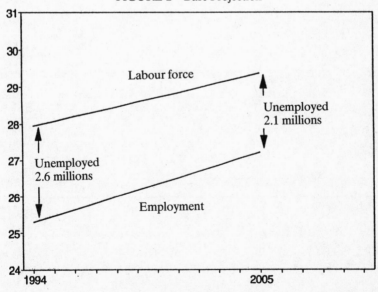

© The Political Quarterly Publishing Co. Ltd. 1995.

FIGURE 3   Effect of Special Measures

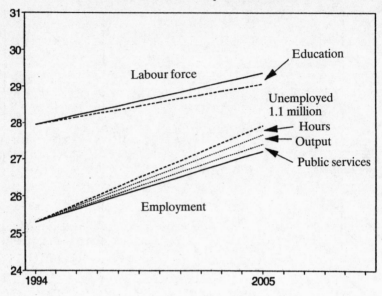

© The Political Quarterly Publishing Co. Ltd. 1995.

© The Political Quarterly Publishing Co. Ltd. 1995. Published by Blackwell Publishers, 108 Cowley Road, Oxford
OX4 1JF, UK and 238 Main Street, Cambridge, MA 02142, USA.

LOCAL DEVELOPMENT ON THE PROGRESSIVE POLITICAL AGENDA

MICHAEL PIORE*

THE purpose of this chapter is to write about local development policy and its place in reforming the agenda of progressive, left-wing politics. I have divided my remarks rather inelegantly into two parts. First, I discuss what local development policy is, or could be. Next I suggest its place on the progressive political agenda.

In the generic sense, local development is any set of policies which focus on the economic growth of a limited geographic region within a broader nation-state. It is different from development *per se*, because such regions are not sovereign. They do not control the flow of goods and services across their borders; they cannot issue money and hence do not conduct monetary policy; their fiscal authority is residual and generally quite limited as well; their basic economic institutions and legal structures are not of their own making. Historically, local development policy has generally consisted of subsidies and tax abatement for industrial location and infrastructure investments ranging from roads to sewers to education and training. These have been the stock and trade of local development authorities. We should probably pay more attention to them: in particular places at particular times they may indeed be critical to economic welfare; but they seem unlikely to hold the key to national economic revival or to the revival of the political fortunes of left-wing forces in national politics.

What makes local development an exciting *new* area of public policy concern, and qualifies it for the place it has on this programme, is the sense that over the last twenty years a fundamental change has occurred in the nature of economic growth in advanced industrial economies. That change has given regional and local economies more independence as a locus of economic development separate from the larger nation state in which they reside and made local development an increasingly autonomous realm of policy.

In earlier postwar decades—indeed from the late nineteenth century and for the greater part of the twentieth—economic development was driven by the logic of mass production. Growth depended upon the economies of scale inherent in the use of highly specialised resources, dedicated capital equipment and narrowly trained semi-skilled workers; these resources produced long runs of standardised products for large,

* Michael Piore is a Professor of Economics at the Massachusetts Institute of Technology.

© The Political Quarterly Publishing Co. Ltd. 1995.

stable, and predictable markets. The key institutions in this development process were the nation state and the large national (and then multi-national) corporation. The nation state created and maintained the background conditions of stability and uniformity in the overall economy necessary to sustain mass production through its monetary, fiscal and regulatory policies. The corporations operated to insure these conditions in the particular markets for their own products while, internally, their hierarchical, bureaucratic structures ensured that the highly specialised components of the production process were well-coordinated and controlled. Local development policy was under these circumstances about where in the national territory the large corporate units and their dependent suppliers would locate their operations. We made a sharp distinction between the high road of infra-structure investment and the low road of subsidies, tax abatements and wage concessions, but both approaches were basically about attracting businesses. Once the businesses got there, they would decide what to produce, how to produce it, and where to sell it. Business was thus the target and the client of the local policy. This made the development authority hostage to business organisations and their natural ally. Inevitably this set development policy against other local groups and interests, many of which were the allies of the Left.

In recent years, the imperatives of the development process have shifted, and important changes have emerged in increasing the autonomy of regions. The first is the shift toward flexible systems of work organisation as the dominant productive technology and, closely associated with this, the movement away from bureaucratic, hierarchical organisations to neworks of economic agents federated more loosely and in more egalitarian organisational configurations. Geographically compact regions which share a common language and cultural traditions are particularly conducive to the formation and operation of such networks. The second change is the internationalisation of production, modifying the role of the nation state in economic policy, making subnational communities much more dependent on their own resources and their own initiatives. This is true in both a positive and a negative sense. It is true in the positive sense that any local region can make up for deficiencies in its national market by selling in other countries. By the same token, now that national economies are more open to foreign products, local producers do not necessarily benefit from an expansion of domestic purchasing power.

In the new environment, development is about the community finding a place for itself in world markets and thinking about how to turn its particular cultural heritage into an asset in that endeavour. It is no longer a question simply of negotiating among local interests to obtain resources, and then with outside organisations to accept those resources in return for locating facilities in the region. It is more a question of purposeful reflection and debate within the local community. Indeed, the community needs to engage in two different, apparently quite divergent kinds of

© The Political Quarterly Publishing Co. Ltd. 1995.

reflection which ultimately need to be married in some way. One is a reflection on the nature of the community itself. The other is about the outside world in which it must market its products. The new local development policy is thus about how to catalyze these debates and give them direction and momentum.

Policy of this kind does not lend itself to formulas. One cannot easily list a set of programmes which will constitute the components of development policy. Indeed, numerous communities with virtually every programme of which one can conceive are at best only attracting branch plants of multinational corporations. But a range of examples could illustrate the kinds of policies one is trying to generate.

Searching for models

One example involves world tours by small teams of community leaders drawn from different economic and social groups in the local area. The teams are sent out to visit areas which might serve either as models or targets for the community's own development. For models, the teams generally pick communities with a similar resources base and/or economic history. A declining steel region might visit another region where the major producers have gone out of business; a city losing a large automobile plant might visit a metal-working region. For targets, the teams might pick regions which produce products downstream in the production process from the region's own industrial output, but they might more profitably visit international trade fairs where goods and services comparable to those produced at home are on display. At later stages in community development, regions often try to attract international trade fairs themselves. These international touring teams serve at least three distinct purposes. First, they raise the sights and enlarge the vision of the team members. Secondly, they provide material to catalyze a broader debate back home and, equally important, *among* the organisations which the team members represent. Thirdly, the experience of travelling together in a foreign environment helps people from different, often antagonistic, segments of the local community to get to know each other: it breaks down barriers among them and provides a common set of experiences and a shared knowledge base upon which to build a more cooperative relationship.

Other examples reenforce this notion that what is being built is not simply particular resources and expertise, but a shared resource base and a capacity for cooperation. Thus in the old development policies, businesses were treated as isolated units, and when there was actually business development—most policy as noted consisted in attracting outside firms to locate locally—it took the form of financial assistance and expertise transferred from a government agency to a particular client firm. In community economic development, however, the idea is that local businesses should learn to support each other. The role of government is

81

to catalyze that learning process. Thus, in one programme, the government provides facilitators whose role is to mediate between the multiplicity of government agencies with support programmes and put together packages of aid to individual firms. Individual firms cannot apply directly to these facilitators. The facilitators are rather assigned to community-based organisations and available only if local businesses join together to form such an organisation.

In another exemplary programme, the government development agency serves as a referral agency for private consultants; it sometimes subsidises the consulting fees but on a declining scale. It does not provide single referrals. It provides each client with a list of consultants and it encourages new clients to visit other firms in the community which have used those consultants and to compare notes. The agency does the same thing with suppliers and subcontractors. The aim of this programme is not simply to build individual businesses, but to build a broad resource base in the community with a dense set of interrelationships.

In still another example, the development agency has developed a group of contractors who practise group consulting in the sense that psychologists practise group therapy: a number of small businesses in the same or similar industry or, at least, with similar types of business problems, is brought together to review and criticise each other's business practices.

Examples of local development

The broader goal in each local development programme is, however, not so much to aid business individually or in groups, but to identify, or create, some kind of industrial identity for the community as a whole which can serve as the fulcrum for a development strategy, fostering internal coherence and giving it direction in the world market place. One example of how this can occur is the state of Sonora in Northern Mexico. Sonora is a largely agricultural region whose economy, now controlled by large producers, has a tradition not unlike that of the wild west of Hollywood movies. Its people still have the self-image and outward appearance of the cowboys of old. The natural market for Sonora's product is the economy of the North, but it has been cut off by U.S. agricultural standards and until recently focused instead on the protected domestic market. The opening of the Mexican economy and the NAFTA which followed effectively eliminated the region's domestic advantage but without opening the U.S. market. The large producers responded by banding together to export traditional products such as oranges and pork as specially packaged luxury goods to Japan. The region is now debating whether it can capitalise upon the image it has acquired in this process and build upon its 'wild west' tradition in a broad-based development strategy of exporting customised leather goods, such as boots and chaps, and attracting foreign tourists.

An even better example is a region in central Austria which has been

82

© The Political Quarterly Publishing Co. Ltd. 1995.

producing iron ore and metal products since the Middle Ages. The traditional metal industry has recently been in decline. New development, which is still limited, is based on tourism. The region has just launched a new project to create what it calls the 'iron road'. This is a tourist circuit which will constitute a kind of living museum, with operating workshops in a series of local communities along the 'iron road' which vacationers can visit while they are in the region to camp or ski. It is designed to give the old iron industry and the new tourist industries a common community identity, and to use the latter to heighten the visibility of the former as a source of metal-working skills in the world market.

What is common to both of these regions is the way in which a local development strategy grows out of the history of the region and the materials through which its people have traditionally expressed themselves; but at the same time that history is linked to the world marketplace to forge new identities, both personal and regional.

Part II: new policies for new agendas

I do not know how far the world could go in regrouping economic activity and organising it through communities with identities of this kind; nor do I want to exaggerate their importance in the new economic order. Network organisations are developing in other contexts and other ways. Communication and information technologies are facilitating the creation of networks which span geographic areas; extended families of Chinese immigrants have been particularly adept in developing production and marketing networks across national borders. The social and economic structures they are building are remarkably similar to what we know about Jewish banking networks in earlier periods. And, not incidentally, large multinational corporations are replacing, or at least trying to replace, their old bureaucracies with network structures. Japanese corporations, it has been argued, have always been organised in this way. Network organisations are, moreover, not by any means the only strategy through which business is attempting to adjust to the new economic environment. Hence, local development cannot be the only thrust of economic policy, nor even its principal preoccupation. For the Left, I would argue that the kind of local development policy I have just described has a strategic political importance—political in the deep sense of that term—which greatly exceeds its immediate economic significance. It is important, first, because it signals a recognition that the context in which economic policy is formulated has changed significantly in recent years, and that we are engaged in formulating new policies appropriate to that altered context. Secondly, it is important because it provides a forum for developing policies which are consistent with the human values which the Left represents in the political arena, a forum for highlighting those values, for illustrating how those values differ from those of our adversaries, and for

83

© The Political Quarterly Publishing Co. Ltd. 1995.

demonstrating how the difference is reflected in concrete policy alternatives.

To make this argument, of course, one has to begin with some statement of what those values are. For me, what distinguishes—or at least *ought* to distinguish—progressive politics is a commitment to the integrity of the individual combined with the recognition that individuality is realised within a social context, through interaction with other people. The process through which individual identity emerges is thus one with the process through which community identity develops. The preeminently human capacity from this point of view is speech, the essential human creation is language, and the proto-typical human activity is *conversation*.

The commitment to a world in which we are able to realise ourselves as individuals in a social context is threatened today—in a certain sense, it is threatened always—on two sides. In the past the principal threat has come from traditional conservatives committed to a concept of community so encompassing that individuals are completely submerged in the larger social entity. In recent years, and arguably throughout the history of economic policy, the major threat is neo-liberalism.

Despite the distinctive set of values with which progressive politics is associated, progressive economic policy has been developed in the shadow of liberal thought and in very large measure in reaction to it. Our principal target has been the liberal vision of the economy as composed of equal individuals interacting with each other as autonomous actors in a competitive marketplace whose parameters are beyond the control of any single person or institution. We were quite successful in combating this vision in the immediate postwar decades; indeed, given the forces arrayed against us, one might argue even in the latter half of the 19th and early 20th century. But our success derived from the fact that the liberal vision contrasted so sharply with the self-evident reality in the era of mass production. Economic development clearly fostered large bureaucratic corporate enterprises. These enterprises organised and controlled the markets which in liberal theory were supposed to control them. They led to an organisation of productive activity in which individuals were subject to strict hierarchical control that allowed very little room for autonomy and creativity: this led to a sharp dichotomy between owner and managers on the one hand, and workers on the other. The quality of life among the working class allowed almost none of the political liberty and individual autonomy which liberal theory suggested the competitive market would provide.

The economic policies which the Left successfully pursued were designed to assert social control through government action over the concentrations of private power, and to redress the imbalances of income and political power to which they gave rise. To gain acceptance of these policies, we played upon the gap between liberal vision and economic reality: liberalism appeared more of a veil designed to hide the privileges of the system than a theory which elucidated its operation. In the process

84

© The Political Quarterly Publishing Co. Ltd. 1995.

we gave up an attempt to formulate our own vision of the economic order, a vision consistent with a different concept of individuals and of human self-realisation. Proposals to reorganise the productive apparatus along these lines came increasingly to be dismissed as 'utopian'.

The reorganisation of work

The changes in the economic environment which have created the space for the kind of local development policy I have just described have been associated with much broader changes in the capitalist order. The corporate enterprises which dominated the industrial landscape in the postwar decades are increasingly under threat from international competition; many have been driven out of business altogether or forced into mergers to survive; fewer and fewer of those which remain seem in any obvious sense to control the markets which determine their fate. Within those enterprises which survive, work is increasingly being reorganised in ways which break down the distinction between managers and the rank-and-file force and which call into question the working class as a social and political category.

I know that many of my colleagues on the Left argue that those changes hide vast concentrations of economic power which still control the larger system, that corporate enterprises and their managers still and have always exercised control. Even if this were indeed the case—even if the economic reality were essentially unchanged—the political reality is not. The space in which the economic policies of the Left were originally formulated and gained their plausibility has been covered up. A competitive market economy has once again become a plausible vision of how the system might operate. The failure to achieve that vision is now attributed to the very policies and institutions which were created to correct its past abuses. Our commitment to our traditional economic programmes thus leaves us defending a set of policies which are arguably irrelevant to the present economic reality; which at any rate have lost their forensic value in the political process, and which I remind you were always basically designed to bring the system more in line with the values of a liberal individualism to which the Left did not subscribe.

If the new economic environment is very different from the environment of mass production, it is equally distant from the competitive market of the neo-liberal vision. The most striking point of conflict between the liberal vision and the new reality is the network organisations and the way in which they depend, not upon autonomous economic actors, but upon the interaction of individual actors embedded in a social network. This is a different kind of attack on the liberal framework of economic analysis, but it is also a much more powerful critique for the Left to make, because it asserts the possibility of an effective economic system built in the pursuit of our own set of values, our own vision of what human beings are and what kind of society they can achieve. Indeed, I would argue that the very

85

© The Political Quarterly Publishing Co. Ltd. 1995.

process of local development in the new environment—the way in which the 'iron road' becomes the vehicle of economic development in Upper Austria, or the frontier tradition becomes the vehicle through which Sonora creates a place for itself in world markets—*is* the expression of human nature which we as progressives value and seek to realise in the economy. The principal value of new possibilities for local development is that they provide an opportunity for processes of this kind, and it is for this reason that I would make them central to the new progressive agenda.

There are secondary reasons as well. First is the fact that local communities are not the only structures in which network organisations can be embedded. They can, as already noted, also emerge in large corporate enterprises. Local communities tend to lend themselves to democratic control in a way that corporate networks do not, and this constitutes a strong argument for policies designed to develop the communal framework and push it as far as it will go.

New network organisations—as I am sure I do not need to remind you— are not the only ways in which business has responded to the pressures of the new international environment. That environment has unleashed incredible labour market pressures in the form of unemployment at home and easy access to low wage labour abroad, and this has enabled many companies to compensate for the deficiencies of existing organisational structures and productive technologies by reducing wages and working conditions. Even the new networks have sought to cut out and subcontract operations which do not require skill, cooperation and loyalty, creating a kind of secondary economy which services the dynamic, flexible systems in the core but does not participate in the networks of which those systems are composed. As a result, the distribution of income and opportunity within the industrial world has widened over the course of the last decade.

The absorption capacity of the emergent economic system appears to be much more limited than that of the old. The logic of the system of mass production was to create and expand the market for its products, drawing more and more people into its orbit as producers and consumers and creating a political constituency within the business community for full employment policies. In the new international order, this constituency no longer exists. As noted earlier, the demand generated by full employment policies at home too easily leaks out to competitors abroad, and foreign markets too often seem a more promising source of demand than domestic economic expansion. We are thus left with a growing number of excluded workers, people often able to command support through the political process in the form of unemployment insurance, early retirement, and social welfare payments, but unable to generate resources to sustain these supports through participation in the economy. These groups are the constituencies of the Left, and left-wing parties have been the principal proponents of programmes which support these newly excluded groups. These, as well as a number of other subordinate and disadvantaged minorities, have been increasingly vocal in recent years. They make

86

© The Political Quarterly Publishing Co. Ltd. 1995.

resources demands through the political process, but are essentially divorced from the economic system. The capacity of the economy to support all of these groups is limited, and the only viable solution over the long run is integration into productive activity.

Conclusion

It may take some time to work out how to effectively incorporate these excluded groups. Our major policy instrument for doing so has been equal employment opportunity policy. That policy has had only limited success. To the extent that it goes beyond an attack on discrimination, it is essentially an attempt to impose so many minorities, so many handicapped, so many older workers on private employers by fiat, and those workers are then carried on the payroll without being effectively integrated into the productive process. We do not, in fact, know how to integrate excluded groups into that process, unless it be to draw their members into the 'conversations' through which network organisations emerge and evolve over time. Some local development is about orchestrating these conversations within the community. It provides an opportunity to experiment with modes of incorporating the economically excluded, an opportunity which is not offered in other forms of network organisation.

87

© The Political Quarterly Publishing Co. Ltd. 1995.

© The Political Quarterly Publishing Co. Ltd. 1995. Published by Blackwell Publishers, 108 Cowley Road, Oxford OX4 1JF, UK and 238 Main Street, Cambridge, MA 02142, USA.

THE GOOD CITY AND ITS CIVIC LEADERS

DAVID DONNISON*

In Britain the Left have come to see national governments as the main instrument of social progress. That would have seemed odd to their forbears—Victorian and Edwardian radicals who set about their reforming work in the town halls long before they had any hope of gaining power in Westminster. We must rediscover their capacity for innovative civic leadership. Most of the major policy changes which have made this country a more civilised place originated at local levels. The first poor relief, the first hospitals, the first clean water supplies, the first schools and subsidised rented housing for working class families, the first comprehensive secondary education—all were launched locally, sometimes by municipal authorities, sometimes by churches or voluntary agencies, and often in the teeth of opposition from the central government which, years later, was chivvying the laggards to adopt the same policies all across the land.

But this is not a good time to appeal for bold civic leadership from local councillors and their officials who have for years seen the needs of their most vulnerable people growing more urgent while their own powers to meet those needs have been reduced, their revenues have been capped, and their work has been complicated by increasingly elaborate requirements imposed by central government and by increasingly aggressive interventions by quangos, rolling around their territory in politically unaccountable ways like loose canon. Nevertheless, these bleak times for local government make it all the more important to reassert the importance—too long neglected—of places and civic leadership. I shall do that by:

- asking what kind of local society we should be trying to create: what would 'the good city'—or the good village—be like?
- providing some understanding of the powerful tides—economic, social and political—now sweeping us in contrary directions, and their destructive effects;
- outlining strategies which civic leaders can adopt that will help to arrest and reverse these disastrous trends;
- and offering, finally, some broader conclusions.

* David Donnison works at the University of Glasgow. His latest publications include *A Radical Agenda*, Rivers Oram Press, London, 1991; and *Act Local*, IPPR for Social Justice Commission, London, 1994.

© The Political Quarterly Publishing Co. Ltd. 1995.

Civil leaders cannot by themselves transform the course of a society's development. That will call for action to be taken at the national and international levels dealt with in other parts of this book. But the purpose of this chapter is to focus on the things which have to be done at a local level.

The good city

Political movements which are running out of steam often try to drum up support with moral outrage focused on easy targets. So our Prime Minister has told us that it is time 'to get back to basics' and 'to understand a little less and condemn a little more'. People deprived of jobs and social security benefits must, if necessary, beg for a living; but not 'aggressively'. The Home Secretary, casting aside the findings of his own department's research, has asserted that 'prison *works*' and encourages the courts to send more people there. Meanwhile other Ministers have lectured youngsters about drug taking, and told lone parents that they would do better to get, or stay, married.

It is a little too easy to deride and dismiss this ill-judged preaching, coming from a regime scarcely noted for its own moral purity. There *is* more crime than there used to be, and fear of crime has increased more sharply still. Riots, in Beatrix Campbell's telling phrase, 'have become routine'[1] and the world has in various ways become a more brutal place than it used to be. Public concern about these trends is urgent and anyone who claims to be a democrat must take it seriously.

Morality grows out of a social situation. The one does not precisely dictate the other, but for every sociology there are feasible moralities, and for every morality a naturally sustaining sociology. An anecdote will illustrate what I mean. Fifty-one years ago, when I joined the navy, I found myself in a large transit camp where any possession one particularly valued (the hair brush with which my mother had sent me off to war, for example) soon disappeared. No-one helped anyone else. It was a dreary place, like a not-very-open prison. Later, in small ships, I was moved by the comradeship of their crews. There, personal possessions were absolutely safe and people took care of each other. If a man returned drunk from shore, someone would put him to bed and someone else would stand his watch for him rather than expose the ship to danger or a shipmate to punishment. Returning briefly to transit camps between postings, I thought that I had perhaps exaggerated their awfulness. But no: they were as bad as ever. The point of my story is that the people in the ships and the people in the camps were essentially the same men—my fellow citizens behaving in different ways under different circumstances. Conservatives of Michael Howard's cast of mind point out that only a few people become thieves, even in a transit camp; which is true. But it takes only a few thieves to make everyone more anxious and suspicious, and less helpful to strangers.

---

[1] Beatrix Campbell, *Goliath. Britain's Dangerous Places*, Methuen, London, 1993.

© The Political Quarterly Publishing Co. Ltd. 1995.

DAVID DONNISON

The same analysis can be applied to lone parents. When politicians (and ageing sociologists who are forgetting their first-year classes in research methodology) warn us that children raised by only one parent do worse than those raised by two, we have to ask them, first, whether these particular lone-parented families do better or worse than they would have done if compelled to share a home which included the rejected or absconding parent. If we found that their break-up was indeed genuinely damaging, we would then have to ask whether that was the fault of the parents, or the fault of a society which views them with a disapproval that condemns most of them to poverty.

On a Manchester council estate where I was recently working, 51 per cent of the households with dependent children had only one adult in them.[2] Lone parents were the norm. Unlike the two-parent families on this estate who were often housed in attractive houses, most of the loners were placed in vast blocks of flats whose concrete walls failed to keep out the cold and the damp, and whose under-floor heating systems were so expensive to run that a woman remarked to me that 'Anyone handed the key to one of these places is condemned to debt'. No-one living on income support—as most of them were—could afford to keep their child warm and healthy unless other resources were somehow found.

Because some of these women were loyally supported by friends and relatives or were exceptionally well organised people, they managed to get by without breaking the law. But this situation guaranteed that the by-passing of electricity meters, shop-lifting, dealing in drugs, squatting in empty houses, concealment of casual earnings, concealment of male partners—all criminal offences for people living on means tested benefits—would become fairly common. And that meant that these mothers were reluctant to be seen talking to police officers or other representatives of authority for fear that they would lose the friends upon whose help they depended for survival.

Morality in such circumstances has not died. These are, to an impressive degree, loyal, kind and courageous women. Morality has *become* whatever behaviour keeps your child alive and well; and your friends and neighbours, living the same kind of life, understand and respect that code.

Long-term unemployment has similar effects—*re*moralising rather than *de*moralising people. The unemployed do not all commit crimes, but crime rises and falls as long-term unemployment rises and falls.[3] If large numbers of young men are compelled to recognise that they will probably never get a proper job and never have a car of their own, it may not be excusable, but it is certainly not surprising if some of them take other people's cars.

If people living in areas where these practices are most common are left

[2] Department of the Environment, *Hulme Study*, H.M.S.O., 1990.
[3] The evidence is deployed in National Association for the Care and Resettlement of Offenders, *Crime and Social Policy*, London, 1995.

90

© The Political Quarterly Publishing Co. Ltd. 1995.

to cope unaided with their intimidating world, then they will do their best to protect themselves by installing heavy locks on their doors and roller blinds on their shop windows, and by keeping fierce dogs to guard their families and their property. Those steps create an even more intimidating environment. Only collective action which rebuilds a more caring community that offers opportunities for legitimate achievement will enable us to rediscover more civilised practices and traditions. If people are not treated with respect—if life in a transit camp world constantly bruises and humiliates them—how can they respect others?

Pausing to summarise where this argument has got to, we can say that a morality grows out of, and is sustained by:

— *institutions* (council estates and dole queues, for example, which may be well managed or badly managed),
— the *practices* which their participating members engage in (perhaps including the by-passing of electricity meters or the stealing of cars, for example),
— and the collective *traditions* which inform and guide those practices (like not speaking to policemen or not grassing on a mate).[4]

There are always resolute individuals who resist local patterns and develop or retain different practices and traditions: *someone* had to be the first to say that eating people was wrong. But if we are talking about large populations, not lone individuals, any significant change in moral values and the behaviour they sanction must be accompanied by changes in social circumstances—changes, that is to say, in the institutions, practices and traditions which play important parts in our lives. It may be the job of preachers to tell individuals to be good. It is the harder task of politicians and civic leaders to create a world in which it is easier for people to be good and harder to be bad. 'Good' and 'bad' are valuations we ourselves formulate and revise as we go along. For some, religious institutions and practices are important influences on those values. Parents and teachers are other important sources. But values are not independently valid principles which we discover from different and deeper levels of inquiry. Wherever they come from, they must be supported by appropriate social circumstances if large numbers of people are to find them feasible to live by.

It is not difficult to describe the main characteristics we would like to find in our cities and villages. They would provide opportunities for all to develop their talents to the full within a community which tolerates and enjoys all cultures that extend the same friendly toleration to others. Their people would not all have to like each other, but they would treat even their enemies with respect, and there would be none of the fear and contempt which tend to be associated with great inequalities of income,

---

[4] The argument is developed further in David Donnison, 'By What Authority? Ethics and Policy Analysis', *Social Policy and Administration*, 28.1. March 1994, p. 20.

91

© The Political Quarterly Publishing Co. Ltd. 1995.

status or power. Political contention would be robust but honest, and political leaders would be accountable to their people through procedures to which everyone would have equal access. *Social Justice*, the Report of the Borrie Commission on Social Justice,[5] outlines this pretty well. It is not a Utopia. Pain and loss cannot be banished from this world, but they can be more fairly shared, not heavily loaded onto particular social groups—and least of all onto children and young people who are a nation's most precious asset.

Long-term unemployment; constant anxiety about insecurity of work, health, home and personal safety; grave inequalities of income, wealth and power; circumstances that make it impossible for large numbers of people to attain opportunities which many of their fellow citizens take for granted—all these make the growth of such a community impossible. So do forces which exclude large groups from gaining a hearing—from participating in the political and public affairs of their society. Many believe that the development of polarised neighbourhoods, setting classes, ethnic groups and age groups apart, also has destructive effects. So perhaps do neighbourhoods where people without strong roots in other networks move about so rapidly that no-one knows who lives next door to them.

Contrary forces and their effects

Formidable tides are now sweeping Britain away from this ideal. These can be briefly summarised. They have been described at greater length elsewhere[6] and in other parts of this book. They start from global trends in the world's economy which are steadily drawing manufacturing work into the countries with labour forces which are orderly, well-educated and cheap. They are carried further by technological changes which are eliminating much of the less skilled work and making many other skills obsolete; and then further again by organisational changes which are stripping out routine jobs and middle ranking layers of management. To these world-wide trends are added more local influences, like the ending of the Cold War and the resulting collapse in the demand for armaments—one of the few sectors in which Britain still had some comparative advantages.

As a result, since about 1972, the long-term tendency of capitalist economies slowly to move towards more equal distributions of income has been reversed. Wages are growing more unequal as those of lower paid and marginal workers drop further behind those of workers well

[5] *Social Justice: Strategies for National Renewal*, the final report of the Commission on Social Justice (the Borrie Commission), Vintage, London, 1994.
[6] Richard Wilkinson, *Unfair Shares*, Barnardos, Ilford, 1994. The Borrie Commission, *op. cit.*, Chapter 1, and *The Justice Gap*, Institute of Public Policy Research, London, 1993. David Donnison, *Act Local, op. cit.*

92

© The Political Quarterly Publishing Co. Ltd. 1995.

established in the core of the economy. Unemployment and *non* employment (which includes people describing themselves as sick, early-retired or inactive) have increased, as if by a ratchet effect: each peak in the depths of recessions exceeding the previous peak, and each trough at the top of the intervening booms also exceeding the previous one. And more and more of the unemployed have been out of work for very long periods.

The resulting poverty is loaded particularly onto children, young people and those who rear them—the families depending on lower paid workers, unemployed people and lone parents. One in every three British children is now growing up in what the European Union defines as poverty—that is, with an income less than half the average for families of the same size in the same country. The good things which are happening in an economy that is still slowly advancing tend to be concentrated in the same households, and the bad things in other households. Thus we have more families with two or more earners and more with none; more youngsters passing examinations and going on to universities and more who are excluded from school as unmanageable; more families buying their own homes and more becoming homeless.

Differences in living standards between city neighbourhoods and between regions of Britain, which for a long while were declining, are now increasing again. Poverty in a neighbourhood where most people are poor drags people further down than poverty in more affluent neighbourhoods: the public and commercial services tend to be poorer both in volume and in quality, the jumble sales offer less—even the tomatoes cost more.

These divisive economic and social trends have been given a further push by political decisions. The tendency to growing inequality has been savagely sharpened since 1985, and the main factors contributing to that development have been changes in taxes and benefits, both of which have taken more from poorer people and given more to richer people. When the Chancellor of the Exchequer said that a rise in unemployment was 'a price well worth paying' to bring the nation's finances under control, he was making clear to whom the Government would give priority when choices have to be made between the interests of those in the core and those on the margins of the economy.

Taken together, these trends are producing a scandal of historic proportions. Nothing quite like it has happened before, and the effects are clearly visible. Richard Wilkinson has summarised many of them.[8]

- More families are breaking up.
- The proportion of children on Child Protection Registers has increased dramatically.
- The numbers of children under ten in public care have also increased.
- The numbers of pupils expelled from primary and secondary schools have increased.

[7] Richard Wilkinson, *op. cit.*
[8] Richard Wilkinson, *op. cit.*

93

© The Political Quarterly Publishing Co. Ltd. 1995.

- Three studies have shown a decline in reading ages among 7–8-year-olds, concentrated at the lower end of the ability range.
- One study shows a similar decline in mathematical attainment.
- There has been a disturbing increase in the numbers of homeless youngsters, particularly around the ages of 16 to 18.
- There has been a big increase in suicides among young men between the ages of 15 and 24.
- Total reported crime and violent crime have both increased dramatically, and so has the fear of crime.
- There have been major increases in the numbers of young drug offenders and in deaths from solvent abuse.
- Mortality rates for men and women between the ages of 15 and 44–who include the parents of many of these youngsters—have begun to rise.

Most of these changes began, or proceeded faster, from about 1985 when the trend to greater inequality was sharpened. Some of the figures may owe a good deal to changes in recording practices, but together they leave no doubt that there has been a crushing increase in hardships for many children and young people and those who care for them. They show, too, some of the effects of these stresses—effects for which the whole society ultimately pays a heavy price.

Part of the price we pay for growing inequality is measurable in money: the costs of keeping more people alive on social security benefits and doing without the taxes they would rather be paying in a proper job, the costs of keeping more people in hospitals and prisons and taking more children into public care, the costs of higher insurance premiums against burglary and car theft. Less easily measurable but more pervasive and damaging are the costs of lost hope. The millions in the dole queues threaten the jobs of all in the more exposed parts of the labour market, making it easier to exploit workers and cut their wages. Half the British Government's famous deficit is accounted for by the cost of unemployment—in social security payments and lost taxes. While that continues, every Chancellor of the Exchequer must fight to cut public expenditure. Meanwhile, every trade union is likely to be suspicious of proposals to make it easier for people with physical or mental handicaps to support themselves, for prisoners to earn money and recompense their victims, for students to work their way through college, for pensioners to keep working if they wish to, and for many other things which would make the world a better place. Widespread anxiety and loss of hope for the future depress a whole society, showing up in poorer health and earlier death.

Crime provided a way into this discussion because, of all the things happening to us, it most obviously concerns a lot of people. But there is no simple causal link between poverty and crime. Some of the most outrageous crimes are committed by rich people. The key factor is not poverty but inequality. It clearly affects health and life expectancy. In the

94

© The Political Quarterly Publishing Co. Ltd. 1995.

more developed economies, life expectancy depends not on the average level of incomes, but on their distribution: the more equal societies being those in which people live longest. Countries which grow more equal over time (like Japan) climb the league tables for longevity, while those which grow more unequal (like Britain) slip steadily down to that league's second and third divisions. The deficit in life expectancies seen in more unequal societies arises from nearly all causes of death,and it affects not only the poorest people but all income groups up to the average for the nation concerned. It is therefore likely to be due to a general erosion of immunity which afflicts a lot of people in the more insecure, divided and brutal societies. 'Inequality', we can say to at least half our fellow citizens, 'damages your health'. But the damage does not stop there.

A woman sacrifices a good deal if she ties her life to a man's. In return, she used to receive a regular wage packet. In places where there are very few men in a position to provide that kind of support it is not surprising if marriage and stable partnerships are growing less popular and if children suffer some of the effects of those changes. William Julius Wilson has traced these patterns in the United States' ghettos, showing how marriage rates decline as opportunities for regular work disappear[9] and similar patterns can be seen in poverty-stricken neighbourhoods here.

Factors which exert so profound an influence on health and demography must have many other effects too, and particularly on children and young people who are at more vulnerable, formative stages of their lives than the rest of us. Wilkinson's data show what some of these effects are, but much more research will be needed to explain exactly how they work. Crime and a wide range of incivilities are among them, prompted probably by the lack of opportunities for legitimate achievement, a growing sense of injustice, loss of respect for others and perhaps the sheer boredom of poverty. But although crime inflicts painful loss and fear on other people, it may not be the worst of these effects. Apathy, alienation, depression, addiction and domestic conflict may be as damaging, and sometimes more so.

The response of civic leaders

These social trends have political implications. The doctrines of radical movements in the western world were hammered out during the first half of the twentieth century. The British Labour Party did not adopt a distinctively socialist identity till 1918, and many of its more familiar aspirations took shape later still. During these years the main conflicts in British society divided the working class from the middle class, the manual from the non-manual workers. That frontier was, roughly speaking, the dividing

[9] William Julius Wilson, *The Truly Disadvantaged*, University of Chicago Press, 1987, Chapter 3.

95

© The Political Quarterly Publishing Co. Ltd. 1995.

line between those who used public transport and those who hoped to own a car, those who rented homes all their lives and those who hoped to buy one, those who used public call boxes and those who hoped to have a telephone in their own homes, those who relied on friendly societies, social insurance and hospital outpatient clinics for their medical care and those who paid their own doctors, those whose children get a free education and left school early and those who paid school fees and hoped their children would go on to college. No wonder politics was class-based!

Although many families led grindingly hard lives during these years—as recorded in the great poverty surveys[10]—most of them were not excluded from the mainstream of their own society in the way that so many are today. They were working class people passing through the troughs in a lifecycle of alternating hardship and relative comfort which particularly afflicted them in childhood, early parenthood and old age. But they remained rooted in working class streets and usually in working class jobs. Through the Labour movement which they created, in alliance with liberal groups in the middle class, they eventually regulated working conditions and minimum wages, achieved full employment, and built a 'welfare state' that protected them from the worst hardships.

That edifice was built on an informed but powerful alliance, articulated through the Labour movement, between working people and the staff of the public services on which they depended. In ward and branch meetings the staff joined forces with their customers, sharing with them a common interest in developing and protecting the 'welfare state'.

Today there are neighbourhoods where that alliance has broken down—some of them landscapes of despair, abandoned by private enterprise and ill-served by public enterprise, where few people have regular work and every family with any choice in the matter is hoping to move out. Most of the working class are now home owners, many with motor cars and telephones, and children in universities. Some pay for their own health care. But they do not live in these neighbourhoods. If they work there, the unions who represent them do not speak for local residents. Officials on the far side of public service counters relieve and regulate the natives, but grim jokes capture the colonial relationships between them: the Mau Mau probably told much the same stories.

'What do you call a thousand dead housing officers?'
'. . . a start?'

If the Labour Party were speaking for the underdogs, such neighbourhoods ought to be its heartlands. The movement is now driving the Conservatives right out of the cities in which they stand—major cities, like

---

[10] See, for example, B. S. Rowntree, *Poverty: a Study of Town Life*, Macmillan, London, 1901; *Poverty and Progress*, Longmans, London, 1941; and, with G. R. Lavers, *Poverty and the Welfare State*, Longmans Green, London, 1951; and A. L. Bowley and A. R. Burnett-Hurst, *Livelihood and Poverty*, King, London, 1915.

© The Political Quarterly Publishing Co. Ltd. 1995.

THE GOOD CITY

Manchester, Leeds and Glasgow, which had Conservative majorities not so long ago. But it is in these wards that election turn-out and party membership are often lowest, and Labour often loses seats to the Liberal Democrats (in Tower Hamlets, for example) or to the parties of anger— Militant in Glasgow's Easterhouse, Sinn Fein in West Belfast and the B.N.P. in the Isle of Dogs. When, for understandable reasons, the larger parties gang up against these interlopers, that teaches a lot of poor people that political activism is yet another way of getting yourself excluded from mainstream society. The situation is now serious enough for Labour to have called a conference[11] of its own activists from such wards to consider how the Party's credibility can be re-established there.

These patterns are more than a threat to one political party. They reflect new and deeper social divisions in what the Germans have called a 'two-thirds-one-third society'—divisions which are destroying hope among a large segment of the rising generation and posing Yeats' question, 'What rough beast, its hour come round at last, slouches towards Bethlehem to be born?'

Can civic leaders do anything to arrest and reverse these trends? Much of the action required to bring unemployment down and to provide an adequate income for those who can no longer return to work has to be taken at national and international scales. But if we wait for our political friends to capture power in Westminster before trying to do anything about these deepening divisions, those friends—with no working local models to give them the confidence to act—will scarcely know what to do.

This is not the place to set forth a programme for the next local elections, even if I were qualified to do that, but it may be possible to sketch the outlines of a strategy already developing in initiatives up and down the land. Those I shall quote may not be best or typical practice: they are simply those I happen to know about, and may therefore over-represent Scotland, the country I know best.

If the social fabric is disintegrating, we need to know where it most urgently needs repair. It is clear that children, young people and their parents bear the brunt of Britain's growing poverty. Every county and major city should keep track of their progress and report every year or two on what is happening to these youngsters. Richard Wilkinson's list of disasters, quoted earlier, might form the starting point for such a record. What is happening to infant and maternal mortality and child health? How are children doing at school? How well do they read? How many are truanting?—or getting expelled? What are their housing conditions? How many become homeless? How many are convicted of offences?—or incarcerated in institutions of various kinds? How many gain various qualifications and jobs?—or remain out of work? Most of this information is already available in the files of Health and Police Authorities, schools, housing departments, social work and employment services. More

[11] On December 3rd 1994 in Manchester.

97

© The Political Quarterly Publishing Co. Ltd. 1995.

difficult will be the task of persuading these bureaucracies to adopt the same areas for statistical analysis, so that the progress of different neighbourhoods can be compared. (But Edinburgh is working towards that objective.) We also need to compare the progress of different ethnic groups, and groups with different disabilities, and—as more local authorities take up the task—the progress of different cities and counties. Armed with information of this kind—far more relevant for policy than figures for hospital waiting lists and pass rates for different schools which now attract so much attention—it will be easier to focus resources on the people and places in greatest need.

From the educational priority areas and community development projects of the 'sixties and 'seventies to the single regeneration budget of today, British governments have remained convinced that problems of deprivation can be solved with special, one-off projects focused on defined areas for limited periods of time. But the crisis we face is too deep-seated to be tackled successfully in this way. Areas and groups with special needs require continuing help which can only be given by building the necessary priorities into mainstream programmes and their budgets. Strathclyde Region, soon to be disbanded, has probably gone further and for longer than other authorities in its attempt to achieve that. The city of Nottingham is setting about the task too.

Getting people who want to support themselves and their families back into work will call for nation-wide action on investment, training, social security benefits and other matters. But even if such a programme succeeds, there are now some neighbourhoods and groups in every major city which have become so excluded that special steps will have to be taken at a local scale if they are to have a chance of getting back into decent jobs. That will require forward planning capacities for cities and counties, and for major areas of stress within them, to identify future opportunities for work which can be foreseen, to train people in advance for them and build up their confidence, to provide good child care services for those who will need them, and to get employers committed to recruiting these people.

Gaining the support of corporate bodies in the public and the private sectors for programmes of this kind is a vital part of the civic leaders' role. There are amongst them people who understand that if they want to attract skilled workers, customers, students—anyone with some choice about where to go—then the reputation of the place in which they work for safety and civilised order, for skills and cultural resources and for the general quality of its environment will be one of their greatest assets, or, if not, one of their greatest liabilities. They have an interest in improving these things. (Business in the Community has helped some firms to recognise this. Meanwhile Liverpool University set about trying to play a constructive part in the life of its city, and particularly in Toxteth, the inner city neighbourhood in which it stands—and found that within two years its bill for broken windows had halved.)

© The Political Quarterly Publishing Co. Ltd. 1995.

Those who live in the most poverty-stricken neighbourhoods include a lot of people who are temporarily or permanently out of the labour force: lone parents, people with disabilities, pensioners and so on. For them, a good welfare rights officer will be more helpful than opportunities for work. The heads of these services in Lothian and Strathclyde Regions agree that an experienced, full-time member of their staff should secure about £150,000 a year in benefits of various kinds to which poor people are already entitled. Most of this money comes from the national, not the local, tax-payer. Harvesting about ten times their salaries, this is a far more cost-effective way of increasing the incomes of poor people than any other form of public expenditure.

Many of the programmes designed to help excluded people are focused on particular areas, but some of the needs to be met are scattered across the map, not concentrated in any particular neighbourhood. Some authorities have helped such groups to escape from philanthropic modes of provision which can be demeaning by treating their needs as a human rights issue. In some places ethnic minorities have gained a voice which cannot be disregarded. The recognition which some of the London Boroughs have given to women's groups and to gay and lesbian groups follows a somewhat similar strategy. Strathclyde's support for 'disability forums' provides another model, bringing together people with various kinds of disability, giving them plentiful information and advice about local meetings of every sort, and taxis to get them to any they wish to attend. They are beginning to make an impact on many services.

Every opportunity should be taken to devolve power to people prepared to manage their own services and projects: community-based housing associations, management cooperatives and full ownership housing cooperatives, credit unions—some of which have added innovative services to their basic task of helping people to save and borrow money at honest rates of interest—old people's clubs and youth clubs . . . these are among the best known versions of the strategy. Liverpool offers some striking examples. They tap the knowledge of people, too often neglected, who have authentic experience of the problems to be solved. They can make the professionals more accountable to those whom they are supposed to serve. They may help to create a sense of community where none existed before. More ambitious are the partnerships between local communities, the state and the private sector, set up to plan and manage the renewal of deprived urban areas. Proposals for developing these more extensively, derived partly from experience in Birkenhead, are made in the Borrie Report on *Social Justice*.

Volunteers and locally recruited staff who work in these enterprises need about as much training and support as the professionals employed in more conventional projects, although this has to be provided in different ways. There is no magic about 'community': the age-old tasks of government have still to be performed—accounting for public money, providing valid successors when old leaders retire or are discarded, dealing fairly

99

© The Political Quarterly Publishing Co. Ltd. 1995.

DAVID DONNISON

with competing customers or competing staff, ensuring that the aggrieved have proper rights of appeal, and so on.

Another development designed to attain some of the same aims of creating a more user-friendly, accountable and participative style of governance can be seen in decentralised, multi-service offices, located in the small neighbourhoods they serve. To these, some authorities have attached representative neighbourhood councils of various kinds which may have a small budget to spend. Islington and (until the Labour Party recaptured it) Tower Hamlets probably had the boldest versions of such a decentralised system. Manchester, too, has set up interesting initiatives of this kind in certain parts of the city.

There are many other projects and places where a new politics of poverty is stumbling into life. Little has been said here about education— for long somewhat over-valued as an instrument of social change, and then for twenty years neglected. It re-emerges as a front runner in the Borrie Report which suggests how the life-long need for learning in an economy which changes increasingly rapidly can be met.

The need for safety—the starting point for the discussion presented here—must also be taken seriously. Salford and Scotland's Central Region are among the authorities which are developing successful, community-based approaches to that task. Central Region are finding that much of the anxiety to which their police have to respond arises from yet another form of deepening social division—conflicts between youngsters and older residents living in the same neighbourhoods. They can be resolved only if a more encompassing sense of community is rebuilt. The Region and its police are devising interesting ways of doing that.

Conclusion

The main strategies for local governance explored in this article can be summarised in a few words:

* Proposals for monitoring what is happening to our children, youngsters and their families—the people most exposed to hardship in an increasingly unjust society—and for giving their needs priority in the development of mainstream services.
* The growing emphasis on economic development to provide opportunities for people to make a living in a rapidly changing economy—and hence also on local economic forecasting, education, training, and child care.
* The drive to develop more open, democratic, accountable, community-based forms of service: some owned or controlled by their users; some delivered from decentralised, user-friendly offices whose staff identify more closely with the communities they serve; and some developing as

100

responses to more robust, rights-based assertions of needs by potentially vulnerable groups.

Together, these strategies attempt to rebuild alliances between civic leaders and the more vulnerable of their citizens, and to recreate a shared sense of mutual respect and concern in badly fractured, increasingly divided communities. I am doing little more than reporting what I have learnt from people working at local levels in many parts of the country to develop these ideas. Their efforts are brave, but cannot take us much further unless we reinvigorate the whole machinery of local governance.

The experience of cities in many parts of the Western world[12] shows that those which cope most successfully with rapid economic and social changes can be found under widely varying regimes—Hamburg, Pittsburgh, Rennes are perhaps among the stars—but they all have a strong group of local citizens with a shared vision of their city's future who work together, communicating with their own local citizens, with leaders of the private and voluntary sectors, and—on behalf of all of them—with higher levels of government. I have called them civic leaders, which is a deliberately vague term, for different people play this part in different societies. In this country, local politicians and their key officials usually have central roles to play, but others—in the private sector, the media, the churches, the universities, the ethnic communities—may also be important players.

To give such leadership effectively, they need more freedom of manoeuvre than is now permitted to British local government, which should eventually have a power of general competence to do anything which is not illegal, as is commonly found among other members of the European Union. That power will mean little, unless local authorities have larger responsibilities for raising their own revenues. The quangos may survive, but they must be brought into closer alliance with democratically accountable authorities which have a leading role within their own cities.

As these strategic questions are sorted out, it will become clear that the new emphasis on community-based and rights-based patterns of governance does not replace more traditional forms of authority. The new patterns will only operate fairly, reliably and accountably within a framework of broader-based civic leadership accountable to the whole city or county. Likewise, councillors and their officials will find that they speak with greater authority and have a better understanding of the problems they are dealing with if they are strongly rooted in the groups and neighbourhoods they serve.

If they are to claim their proper role within a wider group of civic leaders, councillors must lay down standards for their own work and demonstrate that they adhere to them. Incompetence, idleness and sleaze are not confined to Westminster. Such a statement should deal with things like the frank disclosure of members' private interests and the making of

---

[12] Dennis Judd and Michael Parkinson, *Leadership and Urban Regeneration*, Sage, London, 1990.

101

© The Political Quarterly Publishing Co. Ltd. 1995.

clear distinctions between these and their public interests, regular attendance at Council and committee meetings, the holding of regular surgeries at well-known times and places, reporting back to party members and the wider electorate—and much else beside. It is to the credit of the Scottish Labour Party that it is working on just such a statement which will soon be made public.

© The Political Quarterly Publishing Co. Ltd. 1995.

© The Political Quarterly Publishing Co. Ltd. 1995. Published by Blackwell Publishers, 108 Cowley Road, Oxford OX4 1JF, UK and 238 Main Street, Cambridge, MA 02142, USA.

RE-INVENTING CITIZENSHIP: THE ROLE OF FAMILY POLICY

PATRICIA HEWITT*

THE inclusion of family policy in a discussion of how to re-invent citizenship is itself significant, since the relationship between thinking about 'family' and thinking about 'citizenship' has not always been easy. Classically, citizenship has referred to the participation of men within the public sphere. Although that participation was dependent upon the private infrastructure provided by women within families, the connection was often not made, nor its implications for citizenship explored. The feminist critique of classical theories of citizenship has challenged both the taken-for-granted provision of the conditions of public participation and the invisibility of women within the public sphere. In an early effort to claim social recognition for the value of private work, Eleanor Rathbone, for instance, argued the case for family allowances (now, child benefit) as a 'badge of citizenship' for mothers. The point that needs to be stressed for this discussion is that it is not possible to 'reinvent citizenship'—any more than it is possible to reinvent family policy—without allowing a central role for gender.

Instead of considering citizenship and family—public and private—as separate spheres, however, I want to consider the family as the *first* social institution which we all know. Families provide the place where, in our first relationships with other people, we each become individuals; the place where we first learn—or fail to learn—how to become good citizens of the wider community or, more accurately, the wider communities within which we will live. This implies, of course, a rich conception of citizenship, involving far more than simply voting, far more than exercising rights, more even than accepting responsibilities which are legally mandated upon citizens, such as paying taxes. It implies instead a powerfully-felt sense of responsibility towards fellow members of our communities and towards future members of our communities, a commitment to an ethic of mutuality.

Although an adult's life is rarely the inevitable product of childhood experience, the chances of children growing up to become good citizens are profoundly affected by what happens within families, between parents, other adults in the family and children; by the ability of family members to engage within the wider society and economy; and by the nature of the

* Patricia Hewitt was the deputy chair of the Commission on Social Justice. Now director of research for Andersen Consulting, she was formerly director of the Institute for Public Policy Research. She is the author of *About Time: The Revolution in Work and Family Life* and of various pamphlets and articles on family policy.

social and economic environment within which families find themselves operating. In this article, I shall consider the nature of the changes taking place within family structures and their causes; the consequences of those changes, particularly for children; and the implications for policy.

No-one can fail to be aware of the changes taking place within family structures. Although they are particularly marked within the United Kingdom and other Anglo-Saxon societies, similar changes are taking place in most of the industrialised world. Nonetheless, the speed of change is often exaggerated and its nature misunderstood. Although the 'traditional nuclear family'—two married parents living with their dependent children, supported by the male breadwinner and nurtured by the female housewife—is undoubtedly in decline, it has not been replaced by the lone parent family. A current snapshot of families shows that seven out of ten dependent children are living with both their natural parents, two out of ten with one such parent, and the remaining one in a 'reconstituted' family. Amongst the seven out of ten two-parent families, however, the majority are also two-earner families, with a significant minority having *no* earner: the traditional, two-parent, one-earner family is a shrinking group. Furthermore, the two-parent families are increasingly likely to be headed by unmarried couples: in 1992, some 30 per cent of babies were born outside marriage, half of them to couples who were living together.[1] The United Kingdom has one of the highest cohabitation rates in the European Union; since cohabiting couples appear to be at a higher risk of separation than those who marry, this marked increase in cohabitation suggests that the UK's rates of separation and divorce—already amongst the highest in the European Union—are unlikely to decline.

These and related changes within families are the consequences, rather than the cause, of profound transformations taking place within the economic and social structures of industrialised countries. First, the economic restructuring which is gathering pace within the global economy—itself driven by a revolution in the technologies of communication, production and distribution—has produced throughout the Western world a precipitous decline in full-time employment amongst men with low levels of general education (including men with high industry-specific skills) and, particularly, in employment offering a 'family wage'. At the same time employment within the service sectors, including those jobs traditionally regarded as particularly suited to women, have increased. Secondly, women have begun to claim for themselves—in Ulrich Beck's phrase—'the promise of liberal democracy', rejecting a lifetime role ascribed, in feudal fashion, by accident of birth as they rapidly increase their participation in education and employment. Thirdly, the technology of fertility itself has opened up to women the possibility of increased control over whether and when to have a child, extending the years during which child-bearing is possible while, at the same time, the years actually

---

[1] P. Hewitt and P. Leach, *Social Justice, Children and Families*, IPPR, London, 1993.

© The Political Quarterly Publishing Co. Ltd. 1995.

spent in child-rearing as a proportion of the average woman's adult life have substantially shrunk. Fourthly, and partly as a result of these three factors, we have seen a radical change in attitudes towards sexuality, fertility and parenthood.

Even this brief summary of the drivers of change within families suggests that they are deep-seated and unlikely to be reversible. As Beck observes, modernisation 'is not a carriage one can step out of at the next corner, if one does not like it.' Any attempt to restore the primacy of the traditional nuclear family would require the displacement of women, not merely from the labour market, but from education as well. Equality laws would have to be abandoned. 'It would have to be checked,' says Beck, 'whether the evil did not begin with universal suffrage: mobility, the market, new media and information technologies would have to be limited or forbidden.'[2] If, however, these broad economic and social changes are not to be reversed, it is all the more important to recognise that their consequences are neither simple nor wholly beneficial. Indeed, in some cases, they are disastrous.

Inequality: the impact of poverty

The labour market effects of economic change are responsible for the growing inequality in income and life chances which, although significant in all the industrialised countries, is most marked in the Anglo-Saxon economies. In this country, where changes in the tax and benefit system have also played a crucial role, the proportion of children growing up in poverty—now one in three—has trebled since 1979.[3] I need not stress here the very close correlation between childhood poverty, poor physical and emotional health, poor housing, and later educational and social outcomes. Commenting on the increased inequality of family incomes in the last decade, Machin and Waldfogel observe: 'the single most important change . . . is the decline of the male breadwinner.'[4] A minority of men— older men whose skills are no longer required, but also younger men who have never acquired marketable education or skills—has effectively been expelled from the economy. The result is a minority of children whose fathers have never had much opportunity to take financial responsibility for them, who are unlikely to engage in their children's emotional and practical care (although, undoubtedly, some unemployed fathers do precisely that) and who may not even live with their (former or present) partner and the children to whom they are father.

The economic marginalisation of poorly-educated young men is undoubtedly connected with lone parenthood among never-married

[2] U. Beck, The Risk Society, Sage, London, 1993.
[3] Department of Social Security, Households Below Average Income: A statistical analysis 1979–1991/2, HMSO, London, 1994.
[4] Stephen Machin and Jane Waldfogel, The Decline of the Male Breadwinner, LSE Welfare State Programme 103, London, 1994.

© The Political Quarterly Publishing Co. Ltd. 1995.

young women. In the USA, William Julius Wilson found that, whereas for young white women, there were as many employed young white men in the mid 1980s as there were in the 1950s, for young black women the ratio of 'marriageable' young black men had declined dramatically, as violent death, prison, drugs and unemployment take their toll.[5] Something remarkably similar seems to be happening amongst the poorer working-class communities in this country: a map of the regional distribution of teenage lone parenthood shows virtually the same concentrations as a map of the regional distribution of young male non-employment. To that we need to add the evidence of the connection between rising unemployment and rising crime amongst young men, and the observation drawn from criminological analysis that the boys most likely to grow into delinquents or criminals themselves are those with one parent (usually the father) involved in crime.

Also we need to consider the impact upon children of changing family structures themselves. Longitudinal studies make it clear that, taken as a whole, children who have spent part or all of their childhood in a lone parent or reconstituted family suffer worse outcomes than children of intact two-parent families. They also suggest that a major cause of those worse outcomes is the poverty in which the majority of lone-parent families live, although at every income level, lone parenthood is a significant factor in itself. Different kinds of lone-parent families, however, produce different average outcomes for children, with the children of widowed parents doing better on some measures than the children of two-parent families, and children who have suffered multiple transitions (for instance, from a two-parent to a lone-parent family, followed by the re-partnering of the lone parent and a subsequent separation, perhaps followed by a further re-partnering and even a further separation) faring worst of all.[6] The evidence strongly suggests that conflict between the parents—including conflict within a two-parent family—is damaging to children, as is the loss of one parent, usually the father, following a separation or divorce. (More than half of all divorced fathers completely lose contact with their children within ten years, and even reasonably regular access will probably mean a significant loss of emotional as well as physical closeness, compared with what went before.) While bereavement is socially recognised, and good memories of a father are usually kept alive by a widowed mother, the emotional needs of children whose parents have separated or divorced (let alone those of children whose parents have never lived together) are little recognised, the child's loss being compounded by conflict and confusion.

---

[5] William Julius Wilson, *The Truly Disadvantaged*, University of Chicago Press, 1987. In subsequent writings, Wilson has upheld his original analysis against various critiques.
[6] Hewitt and Leach, *op. cit.*

© The Political Quarterly Publishing Co. Ltd. 1995.

The conflict of interests

Here we can see clearly a potent source of conflict between the interests of women and those of children. For the woman, divorce may represent liberation from a relationship which was profoundly unsatisfactory, perhaps constricting or clearly damaging. Despite the drop in income which generally follows divorce, women also report a marked increase in their sense of autonomy and psychological health following separation. For the child, unless of course a separation from an abusive father is essential (in which case, the problem of how to deal with the damage to the child has already arisen), the loss of a father at home will almost always be painful and its reverberations may be felt years later in the young person's capacity to achieve emotional and economic independence.

The damaging effects of economic and social change upon children are compounded by a wholly inadequate public policy framework. I turn, therefore, to what the objectives of a modern policy for families should be and how we might begin to achieve those objectives in practice.

The first goal must be to ensure that children's dependency needs are met, enabling them in turn to become independent and dependable adults. Given the broader context of this discussion, it must be stressed again that the relationships in which we participate as children—above all, the family relationships—will shape the way we participate in broader social institutions as adults. The second goal involves the recognition that 'good enough' families—strong families—need strong women who are capable of helping to meet the economic, as well as the emotional, needs of their children. The third goal, correspondingly, requires us to enable and encourage men to fulfil emotional, as well as economic, responsibilities for their families. Thus, a new conception of family policy provides a basis for a rich view of citizenship in which men and women are enabled to participate fully in family, economy and community.

The policy implications of this kind of thinking are considerable, and I shall only attempt to summarise them briefly. First, an adequate policy for modern families will require a new legal framework for family relationships. Traditionally, Britain, like other European societies, has regulated relationships between parents and children within the framework of marriage. Charles Murray, the American sociologist who has popularised the notion that 'illegitimacy' is the source of most modern ills, would of course like to return to that situation, proposing for instance that the right of mother or children to maintenance, and the right of father to access, should be denied to parents who fail to marry. By contrast, Michael Young and A. H. Halsey have proposed in evidence to the Commission on Social Justice a 'family covenant' concerned with the responsibilities of parents for their children, regardless of the status of the parents' relationship itself. Although the Children Act refers repeatedly to the 'responsibilities of parents', it fails to define those responsibilities, and leaves the unmarried mother in most cases with a practical veto over her partner's acquisition of

107

© The Political Quarterly Publishing Co. Ltd. 1995.

joint parental responsibilities, even where the parents are cohabiting. Instead, Parliament should adopt the Scottish Law Commission's proposal for a new legal statement of parents' responsibilities and should decide, after public consultation and debate, whether those responsibilities should apply to *all* parents—including those who are neither cohabiting nor married—or only to some.

A new statement of parents' responsibilities could, in turn, be used as the basis for introducing what psychologist Susie Orbach calls the 'curriculum of emotional literacy' into our educational system, including the framework of how schools themselves are run. Children who from a very early age respect themselves and others, who learn to deal with conflict and anger without resorting to blows, and who acquire a sense of the responsibilities which go with parenthood are far more likely, in turn, to become the 'good enough' parents in which society has such a vested interest. If this were not enough in itself, the skills implied in the ability to form and sustain successful relationships—the skills required for well-functioning families—also happen to be those which, in a modern economy, are increasingly required for successful employment.

Secondly, new policies for families need to focus on fathers. So much of the debate about families—and particularly about family breakdown—is about mothers. The fathers are metaphorically absent from the debate, as well as literally absent from the lone parent family home. There is, however, ample evidence that men want to be engaged fathers, if only employment and social structures made such engagement more possible. From young offender institutions, probation officers report on the success of groups working with teenage men who are themselves fathers as well as convicted criminals: these angry young men, who have generally learnt no other way than violence of dealing with anger, are desperate to offer something better to their children than they themselves received. Such projects need to be extended, of course. It is ironic, however, that men who are concerned about the next generation generally only become involved as children become teenagers, when they encounter men working as secondary school teachers, youth workers, police officers and probation officers. We know, however, from studies carried out in the USA as well as the UK, that high quality pre-school education can substantially reduce the chances of teenage boys and young men ever becoming involved in serious delinquency or crime. And yet in nursery schools, playgroups and primary schools, men are rare indeed and children whose fathers are missing from their lives at home have few opportunities to grow up with strong images of men in their wider lives at school. Male involvement with young children is often resisted by professionals, and by mothers, not least because of fear of child abuse. If we perpetuate the notion, however, that only women can care for children, then we undermine any other effort we might make to involve fathers more actively within their families—and, of course, we undermine any attempt at equal opportunities within the workplace. Difficult though it will be, we need 'positive action' to encourage

108

© The Political Quarterly Publishing Co. Ltd. 1995.

men to take up work with young children, just as in the earlier days of equal opportunities legislation we needed positive action to encourage women to move into engineering.

Thirdly, the debate about 'work and family' similarly needs to be radically recast. For most employers and policy-makers, 'family-friendly' has been synonymous with 'mother-friendly'. New policies—whether maternity leave, career breaks and part-time work, or help with substitute childcare—have been designed to enable women to juggle employment and family. Meanwhile, the male pattern of full-time work has been left largely untouched. But this uneasy compromise leaves women faced with the unenviable choice between investing time in their children at the expense of their employment (part-time work usually being less senior, less well-paid and less likely to lead to promotion), or retaining their careers at the expense of the time they and their children might have spent together. As Rowthorne points out, younger generations of women, with higher educational qualifications, are more likely to remain in full-time employment, with only brief periods of maternity leave when they have children. Even if childcare provision expands very rapidly indeed, however, the new pattern of two parents with two full-time jobs is unlikely to be satisfactory. Unless very substantial amounts are spent (publicly, privately, or through a combination of both), much of the substitute childcare provision will not be good. In the USA, where women are considerably more likely to work full-time than British women, there is growing concern about the 'parenting deficit' which results when both parents are working long hours. In both countries, not surprisingly, women with children and a full-time job are considerably more likely to be tired and stressed than either fathers in employment, or mothers with a part-time job. Even in Sweden, where publicly-funded childcare is of very high quality, there is growing emphasis on offering time to parents as well as nurseries to children: paid leave is now available to either parent for most of the child's first two years, with significant opportunities for part-time work as well, and special incentives to men to use their leave entitlement.

It is time to recognise that the availability of men for full-time employment was itself made possible by the unpaid work performed by women within the traditional family; the decline of that family pattern itself demands a rethinking of the employment model which it supported.[7] An opportunity is provided here by the flexible use of working time which is taking place in all industrial societies, but which is, for various reasons, more advanced in the United Kingdom. Standard, full-time employment is increasingly supplemented by a variety of working time patterns which include, as well as regular part-time work, annual hours contracts, term-

---

[7] For a fuller discussion of the changes taking place in working time in post-industrial societies, see P. Hewitt, *About Time: The Revolution in Work and Family Life*, Rivers Oram/ IPPR, London, 1993.

© The Political Quarterly Publishing Co. Ltd. 1995.

time working, job-sharing and so on. Furthermore, the standard 'male-stream' lifecycle—education, employment, retirement—is giving way to a far greater variety of lifecycle patterns which, for middle-class men, may include 'portfolio' work in their 50s and 60s (for working-class men, full-time retirement is instead likely to be enforced at an early age). Women who have their children young are increasingly likely to return to employment in their 40s and 50s. It becomes possible, therefore, to imagine a world in which different people will work different hours, combining employment with family responsibilities, further education and leisure/retirement in different ways at different stages of their lives. Employment policy—as well as family policy—will demand imaginative attention to the possibility of giving people time off, full-time or part-time, during their working lives.

That brings us to the fourth aspect of a new approach to families: the need to rethink the welfare state. Beveridge's vision of the post-war welfare state explicitly depended upon both full employment and traditional families. He assumed that men in employment would earn a 'family wage' sufficient for the needs of their wives and children as well as themselves. National insurance, in his conception, would fill the gaps left by illness, disability, unemployment and retirement by providing benefit to the man and his dependants in return for the man's contributions. Ironically, the underlying principle of national insurance—benefits in return for contributions—suits the modern world of flexible employment and shifting family patterns far better than the means-tested benefits on which, under the present Government, a growing proportion of families are forced to rely. Both Income Support (the main out of work benefit) and Family Credit (a means-tested supplement to low wages for earners with children) assume a single-breadwinner family, in defiance of the reality that the majority of two-parent families are also two-earner families; and that the best pathway out of poverty is for both parents to be earners. Instead, Income Support and Family Credit, by aggregating household means (as any means-tested benefit must do), create powerful disincentives to partners to keep or take employment. Even more bizarrely, such benefits give adults a perverse incentive to live apart, rather than reduce their benefits by cohabiting or marrying. Effective 'welfare to work' strategies, and a new commitment to families, will require less, rather than more, reliance on means-testing.

As Josta Esping-Andersen has stressed, the post-war welfare state was passive throughout most people's adult lives. It became active only when people were passive, unable for one reason or another to earn a living—or to depend upon a breadwinner—and thus concentrated resources in the early and last years of life. Within post-industrial societies, however, change within the economy and change within families combines to produce almost permanent insecurity and, with it, the need for an intelligent welfare state which can be active throughout people's lives, enabling both men and women to survive and succeed

110

© The Political Quarterly Publishing Co. Ltd. 1995.

through change.[8] The lone mother without a job needs a source of income, of course; but if that is all that the welfare state offers, it condemns mother and children to poverty. Even more than the benefits system and reform maintenance procedures, that mother needs the combination of education, training, help with jobsearch and with childcare which will enable her to take a job with the hours that will suit her family needs; and that, in turn, requires a reformed benefits system which encourages people to combine, if they need to, part-time earnings and part-time benefit. Similarly, if all the welfare state offers the unemployed man is benefits, it risks condemning him to long-term unemployment: in future, anything except a brief interval of unemployment between jobs should become education and training 'leave' designed to open up new opportunities for employment, whether part-time or full-time, or self-employment.

To conclude: there is, of course, far more to the reinvention of citizenship than the reinvention of families. But the new interest in citizenship, if it is to offer more than rhetorical prospects for a renewed Left, will have to engage with families and how men and women lead their lives within families. The Left must, I believe, be unashamedly traditional in its assertion of parents' responsibilities for bringing up children well and of society's responsibility—in all our interests—in enabling parents to fulfil that duty. At the same time, the Left needs to be utterly modern in understanding how real families now live, in an increasingly complex world, and in engaging with the practical and policy implications of that change.

---

[8] For a fuller discussion, see *Social Justice: Strategies for National Renewal*, the final report of the Commission on Social Justice, Vintage, London, 1994.

111

© The Political Quarterly Publishing Co. Ltd. 1995.

© The Political Quarterly Publishing Co. Ltd. 1995. Published by Blackwell Publishers, 108 Cowley Road, Oxford OX4 1JF, UK and 238 Main Street, Cambridge, MA 02142, USA.

EUROPEAN CITIZENSHIP: A PROJECT IN NEED OF COMPLETION

JOHN PINDER*

THE Maastricht Treaty affirmed that every national of a member state 'shall be a citizen of the Union' and 'shall enjoy the rights conferred by this Treaty and be subject to the duties imposed thereby'.[1] The Treaty goes on to list four main rights: to move and reside freely within the territory of the member states; to petition the European Parliament; to vote and stand as a candidate in local and European elections in the member state in which the citizen resides; and, in countries outside the Union in which the citizen's own state is not represented, to enjoy consular protection by the representative of another member state. The list is slim, the more so since the European Parliament had long since accepted the right of petition and the European Community had established the right to move freely throughout it for purposes connected with work.[2] The EC had, indeed, already established a multitude of rights in the economic and related social fields. Typically, however, the diplomats and bureaucrats who wrote the Maastricht Treaty neglected to make clear to the citizens what such rights might be; and it is not generally realised that these rights are transforming the relationships between the peoples of the member states, who comprise a large and growing proportion of the people of Europe.

EC rights: civil citizenship secured through the rule of law

One of the principal strengths of the Community is that it has created what is, following T. H. Marshall's classic analysis, a civil citizenship in so far as it guarantees a wide range of economic and social civil rights.[3] These rights stem from the simple principles of freedom to buy, sell, invest, establish economic activities or seek and obtain work throughout the Community,

---

* John Pinder is a Visiting Professor at the College of Europe in Bruges and Chairman of the Federal Trust. He was Director of the Policy Studies Institute (formerly PEP) from 1964 to 1985. His books include *European Community: The Building of a Union* (2nd edn., 1995) and *The European Community and Eastern Europe* (1991).

[1] Article 8 European Community Treaty as amended by the European Union Treaty.
[2] See Malcolm Anderson, Monica den Boer and Gary Miller, 'European Citizenship and Cooperation in Justice and Home Affairs', in Andrew Duff, John Pinder and Roy Pryce, eds, *Maastricht and Beyond: Building the European Union*, Routledge, London, 1994, pp. 110, 111.
[3] T. H. Marshall, *Citizenship, Social Class, and Other Essays*, Cambridge University Press, Cambridge, 1950.

regardless of frontiers and without discrimination on grounds of national-
ity. This may seem at first sight to respond to a fairly narrow range of
business interests. But that was not the experience of the half million
Italian workers who became employed in Germany in the 1960s, causing
the Italian Communist Party to respond with policies favourable to the
Community and thus giving momentum to its move towards Euro-
communism and, eventually, social democracy. Nor is it the experience of
the tens of thousands of British and Irish workers who now have jobs in
Germany. It has moreover become increasingly evident that the range of
rights is far from narrow, for they cover the whole vast field of economic
activity to which the freedoms to move and to undertake transactions
apply.

The rights would have remained a pious aspiration had they not been
enforced throughout the Community by the rule of law, ensured by what
amounts to a federal judicial system with the Court of Justice in Luxembourg at its apex. The attacks of right-wing nationalists on 'judicial
activism' and on the Community's 'rigid institutions' merely underline the
significance of this. Their narrow field of vision cannot comprehend the
extension of the principles of the rule of law and citizens' rights to apply
across the frontiers of the existing nation-states; and they thus exclude the
effective application of these principles to the large and growing part of the
citizens' lives, with respect to the economy, security and the environment,
that is increasingly determined by transnational forces—not because of
some sinister interests but because interdependence among states is a
fundamental condition of contemporary civilization. Nationalists who
seek to undermine the Court of Justice and the rule of Community law are
in fact trying to drive their fellow citizens up a cul-de-sac that blocks the
way through which these forces can be properly controlled; and some of
them have the gall to do this in the name of economic liberalism. They
should study their Hayek more carefully. In an article advocating what he
called 'inter-state federalism', he wrote that 'the abrogation of national
sovereignties and the creation of an effective international order of law is a
necessary complement and the logical consummation of the liberal programme'.[4] There is indeed no solid guarantee of open markets and level
playing fields without such a rule of law.

The case for the Community and its rule of law has generally been made
in terms of economic welfare. Such integration does indeed respond to the
needs of economies based on modern science and technology.[5] But even if
this may be sufficient justification for the Community, it is not really
fundamental. More significant is the fact that all citizens are equal before
the law for all EC purposes. Instead of relying on diplomacy, and behind

---

[4] F. A. Hayek, 'The Economic Conditions of Inter-state Federalism', in his *Individualism and Economic Order*, Routledge & Kegan Paul, London, 1949, p. 296, reprinted from the *New Commonwealth Quarterly*, V, No. 2, September 1939.

[5] See Paolo Cecchini with Michel Catinat and Alexis Jacquemin, *The European Challenge 1992: The Benefits of a Single Market*, Wildwood House, Aldershot, 1988.

© The Political Quarterly Publishing Co. Ltd. 1995.

that the power relationships between their states, to deal with their disputes, the citizens of different member states can now go to the courts for judgments in matters that concern some of the most important aspects of their lives. Compared with the protectionism and wars that accompanied the preceding system of absolute national sovereignty, this is surely a qualitative leap in political civilization.

The logic of freedom to move and transact across frontiers has led to an extension of the rights beyond the strictly economic. Thus it has been found necessary to require the Community's institutions to respect the human rights and fundamental freedoms as guaranteed by the European Convention and 'as they result from the constitutional traditions common to the Member States'.[6] If the law is to apply even-handedly to all citizens in the Community, it has to have primacy over any of the laws of member states that may contradict it. That is an essential condition of an effective rule of law. But the member states could not be expected to countenance laws that contravened the rights and freedoms guaranteed under their constitutional traditions. So the Court of Justice concluded that the legislation and actions of the Community institutions must respect those traditions and the European Convention to which the member states are all party.[7] Judicial activism that may have been, but certainly justified and in the true interests of the citizens, as the member states recognised when the words cited above were written into the Maastricht Treaty. But even so, the member states declined to do more than put into the Treaty what the Court had already established, though more is required in certain essential respects.

First, Article L of the Treaty confines the jurisdiction of the Court to the Community Treaties, which are amended but not replaced by Maastricht. The Court is not to have jurisdiction with respect to the other aspects of the Union: not the Common Foreign and Security Policy nor, with some possible exceptions, the Cooperation in Judicial and Home Affairs, nor indeed the first few articles of the Treaty, including the one relating to human rights and fundamental freedoms. The Court will certainly continue to require the Community institutions to respect them, as it has done hitherto. But if the member states were really serious about the rights and freedoms, they would submit the institutions to the jurisdiction of the Court for all their actions under the Treaties and would, indeed, agree that the Union itself accede to the European Convention, as the European Parliament already proposed the Community should do in 1979.[8]

Secondly, the European Union Treaty should require that all member states themselves apply the rights and freedoms. It can surely not be acceptable that Community legislators should include representatives of governments tainted by serious violation of rights. The Treaty states that

---

[6] Article F.2 European Union Treaty.

[7] See A. G. Toth, *The Oxford Encyclopaedia of European Community Law: Vol. 1, Institutional Law*, Oxford University Press, Oxford, 1990, pp. 284–7.

[8] *Ibid.*, p. 291.

114

© The Political Quarterly Publishing Co. Ltd. 1995.

member states' 'systems of government are founded on the principles of democracy'.[9] But it fails to specify those principles, even by reference to the rights and freedoms guaranteed by the European Convention. Nor does it indicate what would happen if a member state failed to respect them. The Community took fairly sharp action against, for example, Bulgaria and Romania when they seriously violated human rights. But there is no indication as to what would happen if the latter were member states, which they doubtless before long will be; and the same applies, of course, to any other member state. The Treaty should surely provide for a judicial inquiry if any such violations are alleged, as well as for some sanctions, including eventually suspension of membership, if they are found to have taken place.

Thirdly, the Union, despite the Community's strength in the economic aspects of civil rights, is weak with respect to the political and social rights for which the European Conventic.1 also provides. Yet without adequate rights in these fields too, those already guaranteed will remain at risk, and hence also will the Union's capacity to contribute to the citizens' prosperity and security.

Political citizenship: still underdeveloped

The rule of law without representative government is an anomaly in Europe today. Citizens are accustomed to have laws enacted by their elected representatives as well as to have the executive controlled by them. Laws not so enacted, or an executive not so controlled, are liable to lack legitimacy in the eyes of the citizens, so that when the going gets rough, as from time to time it will, the Community's laws, which have been made for the most part by an opaque process of intergovernmental negotiation, may not have the strength to prevail; and the rule of law on which the whole structure rests will then be undermined.

When the Spanish government in 1989 put forward the concept of European citizenship for incorporation in the European Union Treaty, its main thrust was to overcome the democratic deficit, in particular by giving the European Parliament equal legislative powers with the Council of Ministers.[10] Thus the idea was to endow the Union with what Marshall called political citizenship: giving the citizens the right to take part in elections to bodies with political authority. A majority of member states, including Germany, favoured this; France was lukewarm; Britain against. Since treaty amendments must be ratified by all the member states, the British Government was well placed to block the proposal of co-legislation; and although it did not press its opposition to the limit, the result was an emasculated version of what the Spaniards and others had intended.

Despite the significant enhancement of the Parliament's powers,

[9] Article F.1 European Union Treaty.
[10] Anderson, den Boer and Miller, *op. cit.*, p. 108.

© The Political Quarterly Publishing Co. Ltd. 1995.

Maastricht left the Council as the Community's principal legislature, together with a fairly dominant role in the executive function. How unsatisfactory the Ministers' performance in the Council is liable to be was vividly expressed by Alan Clark in his description of the meetings in which he participated.[11]

> Not, really, that it makes the slightest difference to the conclusions of a Council meeting, what the ministers say to it. Everything is decided, horse-traded off, by officials at COREPER, the Council (sic) of Permanent Representatives. The ministers arrive on the scene at the last minute, hot, tired, ill or drunk (sometimes all of these together), read out their piece and depart.

Inevitably, when Ministers come together for a day or so, perhaps once a quarter, they are likely to leave the substance of decisions largely to their officials, who, if not stationed in Brussels at the member states' Permanent Representations, can at least meet often enough to deal with the substance of the problems. Ministers can, indeed, be quite ignorant about the procedures, as witness Clark's calling the Committee of Permanent Representatives a Council. His depiction of the Council itself has, however, the ring of inconvenient truth. But this truth is not often revealed to the public. Until Maastricht, there was no official report at all of the meetings, even of those at which laws were enacted. It was possible for Ministers to come out and claim that they had voted against, in sufficient numbers to have ensured, had they really done so, that the law in question would not in fact have been passed. Although, following Maastricht, it was agreed that some report should be published, and the Dutch government pressed for a fairly full account, opposition from other governments, including the British, ensured that such reports will be no more than minimal and that the opening of all legislative sessions to the press and public will remain out of the question. As a former senior official in the Council Secretariat has written: 'The nature of the negotiating process inside the conference room means that the work of the Council is likely to remain opaque.'[12]

Neither the officials of the European institutions nor those of the member states are to blame for this state of affairs. It is indeed to their great credit that so many laws beneficial to the citizens have been enacted, even if some legislation has gone too far in centralising detail. But the citizens now need a better way of making European laws; and it is hard to see how this can be achieved without giving legislative power to the European Parliament, so that even though laws still have to be approved by the Council, they must be approved by the citizens' representatives in the Parliament too. The same goes for the control of the executive. At present part of the executive function is retained by the Council, which means in practice by committees of the member states' officials, and part is

---

[11] Alan Clark, *Diaries*, Weidenfeld, London, 1993, p. 139.
[12] William Nicoll, 'Representing the States', in Duff, Pinder and Pryce, eds., *op. cit.*, p. 192.

© The Political Quarterly Publishing Co. Ltd. 1995.

given to the European Commission, usually under the close supervision of those committees. Thus member states' governments, represented mainly by their officials and to a much lesser extent by Ministers, have usurped the powers that, according to the principles of representative government which are fundamental in the member states, should belong to the citizens' elected representatives; and the British government has been the most enthusiastic usurper of them all.

The European Parliament has nevertheless demonstrated its capacity to use such powers, and the Maastricht Treaty gave it more than it had before.[13] The Parliament was given substantial budgetary powers in the 1970s, partly because it discovered, as the Council had failed to do, that over 100 million units of account (the ecus of that period) of agricultural expenditure were not accounted for.[14] Pressed by the Dutch Parliament in particular, the member states agreed that the European Parliament should have more or less equal powers with the Council in respect of the expenditure side of the Community's budget, with, ironically enough, a monstrous exception: agriculture. There, the French government insisted that the Council retain the sole responsibility; and there the Council can hardly be said to have covered itself in glory. The Parliament's claim to have equal power with the Council for the whole budget, including the agricultural expenditure, is fully justified.

The Single European Act established a cooperation procedure which gave the Parliament substantial influence, though not yet power, over the single market legislation; and the Parliament used this to good effect, securing the adoption of over half the amendments it proposed, including a stricter control of small cars' exhausts than the Council, powerfully influenced by the British and French motor industry lobbies, would other-wise have enacted. Following this effective performance, the Maastricht Treaty gave the Parliament a power of codecision with the Council in fifteen fields of legislation, including the single market, the free movement of people, consumer protection and environmental programmes. But although Germany and a number of other member states wanted codecision to be the normal procedure for Community legislation, Britain, Denmark and to some extent France opposed. It was only because the British government rated the question as being of minor importance that John Major conceded the fifteen specific fields in the final negotiation at Maastricht.[15] For the bulk of legislation, the Council, with its opaque inter-governmental negotiations, remains the dominant legislator. For treaties of accession and association and for many international agreements, how-ever, the Parliament has the power of assent, which it has used to insist that agreements provide for certain rights of, for example, the Palestinians.

---

[13] An analysis of the Parliament's powers after Maastricht is given in Richard Corbett, 'Representing the People', in Duff, Pinder and Pryce, eds., *op. cit.*, pp. 207–28.
[14] See Helen Wallace, *Budgetary Politics: The Finances of the European Communities*, George Allen & Unwin, London 1980, p. 105.
[15] Roy Pryce, 'The Treaty Negotiations', in Duff, Pinder and Pryce, eds., pp. 44, 50.

© The Political Quarterly Publishing Co. Ltd. 1995.

The Parliament has used its budgetary powers and legislative rights to gain substantial influence over the Commission. Already in the mid-1980s, the British Permanent Representative wrote that the Commission 'pays a great deal of attention to the Parliament' in drafting legislation, in budgetary matters and in the line it takes in the Council. He observed, moreover, that the Parliament had 'increased its influence dramatically since it was first directly elected in 1979', thus confirming the force of the idea of representative government, in anticipation of actual constitutional provision for it in terms of the powers of the elected representatives.[16] The Maastricht Treaty took an important step towards such provision by giving the Parliament the right to approve—or disapprove—the appointment of the Commission. Used with skill, this right could do much to turn the Commission into a parliamentary executive: a major element in a system of representative government.

Although the British government was quite supportive of proposals to increase the Parliament's power to control the Commission, wanting the Commission to be 'reined in' and recognising that twelve or more separate member states' parliaments were in no position to do this, John Major has subsequently sought to undermine the European Parliament's role. He has asserted that it is 'not the answer to the democratic deficit, as the pitiably low turn-out in the (1994) European elections so vividly illustrated'.[17] He did not comment on the 38 per cent turn-out for the American Congressional elections later in the same year, compared with which the European Union's 56 per cent looks far from pitiable. He went on to denigrate the 'rather incoherent range of parties in the European Parliament, in which fringe, protest and opposition groups are over-represented'. The tilt at opposition groups was understandable, given the Labour Party's massive gains, even if Major did not explain what is wrong with an election that reflects a swing of opinion against the governing party. But the impression of incoherence hardly gives an accurate picture of a parliament in which over 70 per cent of the members belong to the three main party groups, and most of the rest are closely aligned with one or other of them. Major's concern was, however, not so much to paint an accurate picture as to build a case for refusing to accept any further increase of the Parliament's powers as a result of the Intergovernmental Conference to be convened in 1996. He appears to have little interest in applying the principles of representative government at the level of the Union; and the right wing of his party is ferociously against.

This negative attitude towards the European institutions also works against the development of the European civil society in which independent organisations and associations at European level act as both counterweights and supports for the political institutions. The experience

[16] Sir Michael Butler, *Europe: More than a Continent*, William Heinemann, London, 1986, pp. 22, 158.

[17] William and Mary Lecture, given by the Prime Minister the Rt Hon. John Major MP at the University, Leiden, 7 September 1994.

© The Political Quarterly Publishing Co. Ltd. 1995.

of post-Soviet Eastern Europe has been a sharp reminder of the essential role of such a civil society for a democratic polity.[18] The activity of interest groups seeking to influence the Parliament and the Commission and the development of European party groups bear witness to the potential for this counterpart of representative government at the European level. But the more the power remains concentrated in the Council, the more the civil society will remain insulated within the member states, and the less capable the Union will be of supporting democratic European institutions, or its citizens of playing a full part in the control of the processes that comprise a great and growing part of their political environment.

All of which points towards the need for a political citizenship as a complement of the Community's civil citizenship, for which the principal requirement is legislative power for the European Parliament, to which the Commission should moreover be unequivocally responsible. Only then will the citizens be sending their elected representatives to a body with the political authority that the principle of political citizenship demands.

Social citizenship: the need for positive integration

The creation of a customs union or a single market requires the removal of barriers to economic transactions between the member states. For countries the size of those in Europe, this is necessary to give space for the development of the modern economy. But it removes instruments of policy from the governments of the member states and thus reduces their capacity to secure some welfare aims. Hence the need for common policies towards objectives beyond those that the single market itself fulfils. Market freedom across frontiers, sometimes called negative integration, has run ahead of the Union's capacity for the positive integration that would enable it to work more effectively for such objectives and thus make its due contribution to Marshall's third category: social citizenship.

This does not imply carte blanche for the Union to pursue all kinds of welfare objectives. Article A of the Maastricht Treaty rightly affirms that decisions should be taken 'as closely as possible to the citizen'; and many welfare policies are better handled within the member states—preferably, indeed, in a state the size of the United Kingdom, at a regional or local level. Nor should the Union generate policies that do not stand a good chance of success. But unemployment is a common problem to which some common solutions are required. Action by the separate member states is not likely to be adequate, because they do not have all the necessary policy instruments and, given the degree of interdependence, the effects of what they do will spill over into other member states. Thus an optimal policy mix must include substantial action by the Union, as was

[18] See Ernest Gellner, *Conditions of Liberty: Civil Society and its Rivals*, Hamish Hamilton, London, 1994.

© The Political Quarterly Publishing Co. Ltd. 1995.

recognised by the governments when they asked President Delors to produce the White Paper on *Growth, Competitiveness, Employment*.[19]

Much of the Delors White Paper concerns the working of labour markets, which, because the systems vary so much in the different member states, should be dealt with mainly by those states rather than by the Union.[20] But the view that little more needs to be done is dangerously reductionist. The White Paper also contains important proposals for trans-European networks (TENs) in the fields of telecommunications, transport and energy, as well as union policies for technological research and development and for creating a clean environment. The TENs in particular would do much to provide a context in which firms would invest in the economic development that Europeans will need in the 21st century, in particular with respect to a dynamic information society.[21] They would create employment during the lengthy period of their construction. They would establish the physical counterpart of the legal framework for the single market; and they would give major support to the political cohesion of the Union. The TENs should, indeed, help to bind the whole of Europe together, as the single European infrastructure they would create should not be confined within the Union but stretch beyond it into Central and Eastern Europe and the CIS. But the TENs require an essential minimum of financial support from the Union, which the German government has joined the British in being unwilling to allow the Union to provide.

Economic and social cohesion is the name for another set of policies that stem from the need to complement the creation of the single market. The governments of the less-developed among the member states, fearing that they might lose out in competition with the stronger economies in the single market, demanded that it be accompanied by substantial assistance to them through the European 'structural funds'. In order to secure their agreement to the single market programme, the richer member states accepted; and the process was repeated when the single currency project was agreed in the Maastricht Treaty. Thus cohesion is becoming one of the Union's major policies, with expenditure on it due to rise in the 1990s to one-third of the total budget.

The TENs and the environment and cohesion policies are elements in a social citizenship of the Union, in that they contribute to the citizens' right to share in a certain standard of economic and social wellbeing. The extent to which the Union should seek to supplement the social aspects of the welfare state is, however, limited by the principle of subsidiarity. As a general rule, such things are better done within the member states. But

---

[19] European Commission, *Growth, Competitiveness, Employment: The Challenges and Ways Forward into the 21st Century*, White Paper, Office for Official Publications of the European Communities, Luxembourg, 1994.

[20] See for example Paul Teague and John Grahl, *Industrial Relations and European Integration*, Lawrence & Wishart, London, 1992.

[21] See for example *Beating the Crisis: A Charter for Europe's Industrial Future*, European Round Table of Industrialists, Brussels, 1993.

© The Political Quarterly Publishing Co. Ltd. 1995.

there can be justification for Union involvement where the removal of barriers would lead to the undermining of employment protection measures in member states where these are more highly developed. It is generally agreed that the Union should set standards for health, safety and gender equality at work. Beyond that there is contention, as the conflict over the social chapter for the Maastricht Treaty showed. While the principle of subsidiarity should certainly limit further intervention by the Union, the British government's dogmatic opposition to it has done unnecessary damage to the development of the Union's social citizenship.

The political domination by the Council is a hindrance to positive integration in general and to the development of social citizenship in particular. The officials and Ministers who shape its decisions tend to take a narrow view of their country's interests rather than a broad view of the interests of the Union's citizens as a whole. Too often a measure of positive integration that would be in the general interest is blocked by a single member state or a small minority on grounds of *laissez-faire* policy, national sovereignty or merely inertia. Such seems only too likely to be the fate of much of the Delors White Paper. In this, as in many other cases, the citizens' wishes are better articulated by the European Parliament. Thus there is a link between social citizenship, which implies positive integration, and the political citizenship that requires more power for the Parliament, just as there is a link between political citizenship and the civil citizenship. The three together comprise an interdependent whole.

The need to complete the European citizenship

Although the European Community has established many elements of civil citizenship and the Maastricht Treaty has given the concept of European Union citizenship formal recognition, that concept remains seriously unfulfilled: seriously because, without full citizenship, Europeans will lack the solidarity necessary to meet the hard challenges that certainly lie ahead.

To complete the civil citizenship, the Union should accede to the European Convention on Human Rights, bring the Common Foreign and Security Policy and the Cooperation on Justice and Home Affairs within the jurisdiction of the Court of Justice and establish an effective requirement that the member states themselves respect human rights. For political citizenship, the European Parliament, containing the citizens' elected representatives, should have equal legislative power with the Council, and the Commission should be fully responsible to it. For social citizenship, the Union needs an active economic policy to combat unemployment, a strengthening of its cohesion and environmental policies, and a just measure of employment-related social policy. These are the main measures required for a full realisation of European citizenship.

The measures are supported by substantial interests and political

121

© The Political Quarterly Publishing Co. Ltd. 1995.

forces. Civil citizenship with respect to the economy has been strongly promoted by business and by centre-right parties and governments, despite opposition from the harder nationalist right. The centre-left has generally accepted the main programmes, for customs union, single market and single currency, on the grounds that most workers and citizens are likely to benefit. The extension of civil citizenship beyond the economic field has depended more on pressure from the left and, as far as human rights and fundamental freedoms are concerned, on the judicial logic of the Court of Justice.

Political citizenship has had support from the whole political centre on the Continent, with the exception of the Gaullists and most Danish parties. While British Liberal Democrats have been in favour, most Tories and, until recently, most of the Labour Party have been opposed. Despite the large body of support in principle, progress has in practice been gradual, because of the difficulty of shifting deeply entrenched national political systems. There has been progress, however, as the growth of powers for the European Parliament has shown. With Labour and Liberal Democrat support, and with the prospect of a change of government in Britain, British policy in favour of codecision for the Parliament with the Council could tip the scales.

Social citizenship is supported most strongly by the centre-left: in the European Parliament, the Party of European Socialists and about half the Liberal, Democrat and Reform Group. Just as the centre-left has largely accepted the economic aspects of civil citizenship, so many on the centre-right will accept much of the social citizenship. Christian Democrats in particular have tended to be in favour. But the drive for positive integration and social citizenship is more likely to come from centre-left parties and governments.

Among the member states Germany, together with most of the smaller states, has favoured most aspects of European citizenship; France has supported some; and the British government has consistently opposed, save for the important exception of the single market programme, with its contribution to civil citizenship. But the Labour and Liberal Democrat manifestos for the European elections of 1994 were promising. The idea of citizens' rights should surely, if properly expounded, be attractive to British as to most other citizens. Narrow nationalism versus multi-national solidarity is likely to be a principal theme of the political battles to come during the 1990s and beyond: in the British general elections, in the Intergovernmental Conference to be convened in 1996, and in further constitutional conferences, both British and European, that are likely to follow. It is to be hoped that the left in Britain will firmly hold to the side of solidarity. In doing so, it would be true to the tradition that sees citizenship as a universal concept: relevant from the local community, through the region, to the nation-state, and beyond to Europe and eventually to the world as a whole. European citizenship is a practicable next stage in the realisation of that noble idea.

© The Political Quarterly Publishing Co. Ltd. 1995.

© The Political Quarterly Publishing Co. Ltd. 1995. Published by Blackwell Publishers, 108 Cowley Road, Oxford
OX4 1JF, UK and 238 Main Street, Cambridge, MA 02142, USA.

CAN WE ACHIEVE A NEW CONSTITUTIONAL SETTLEMENT?

ANTHONY LESTER*

IF Labour is returned to power at the next election, whether with or without Liberal Democrat support, it will face formidable challenges in undoing the bad effects of so many years of Conservative government. One of the most difficult political problems will be how to replace the centralised and autocratic British State, developed by four successive Conservative governments, with a democratic and plural system of open and accountable government, based on a modern concept of citizenship.

In preparing for the possibility of a government sympathetic to their aims, constitutional reformers across the opposition parties need to think honestly and carefully about how to achieve radical, orderly and enduring change. The huge obstacles impeding coherent constitutional reform in this country are well understood by anyone who has had sometimes to work against the Whitehall grain in previous Labour governments, and by anyone who remembers the political shambles of previous attempts to modernise the British constitution. The obstacles could be overcome, but only by a very rare combination of political commitment, imagination, broad-mindedness, acumen, and good luck.

There is a gathering consensus among reformers within the opposition parties and beyond that what we British citizens urgently need is nothing less than a new constitutional settlement, within the wider context of our membership of the European Union of European citizens and states. The case for radical reform is overwhelming. It has been put on the political map by Charter 88, and has now been largely accepted by Tony Blair, Gordon Brown, Robin Cook, and Tony Wright, as well as by Paddy Ashdown, Roy Jenkins, Robert Maclennan and Shirley Williams, though the strength of that acceptance remains to be severely tried and tested before and after the next election.

The case for reform has been firmly rejected by the Conservative governments which have exercised power since 1979. Tory Ministers and their mandarins understandably regard the idea of new constitutional and legal limits to their wide and convenient monarchical powers and privileges as anathema. Northern Irish affairs apart, they will fight the next

* Lord Lester of Herne Hill QC is a Liberal Democrat peer, a constitutional lawyer, and a Charter 88 Trustee. He was Special Adviser to Roy Jenkins at the Home Office, between 1974 and 1976, and Special Adviser to the Standing Commission on Human Rights in Northern Ireland, between 1975 and 1977.

123

election defending the indefensible status quo with the language of patriotism and national unity. They will also oppose necessary constitutional reforms of the European Union, including any attempt at the Inter-Governmental Conference in 1996 to strengthen European, national and regional democracy and the protection of human rights within the European Union. In opposition, they would fiercely resist every reforming measure taken on the floor of the House of Commons, clause by clause, line by line.

Tony Blair remains agnostic about the vital and indispensable objective of reforming the present unfair voting system for parliamentary, European and local elections. But with that important and, let us hope, only temporary exception, there is support among enlightened political thinkers across the opposition parties for a wide range of related reforms. They are designed to create a plural system of democratic, effective and accountable government based on a modern concept of citizenship and the rule of law.

From subject to citizen

What the reformers aim for is radical and very ambitious: nothing less than a new constitutional scheme which gives the European Convention on Human Rights the same paramount status in UK law as is given to European Community law; which sets legally enforceable limits upon the prerogative powers of the Crown within and outside Parliament; which shifts substantial power from over-centralised Whitehall departments and the unelected 'new magistracy' of quangos to a Scottish Parliament and Welsh Assembly, as well as to English Regional Assemblies (where and only where there is sufficient regional demand for them), and to a renewed system of local government; which makes Parliament more effective, and creates a democratic and regionally representative Upper House; which creates a voting system better reflecting the wishes of electors; which modernises the machinery of justice and improves access to justice; and which promotes greater openness and accountability in government at every level.

Each of these reforms is closely linked with the others, just as they would all be influenced by the shaping of a constitution for European citizens of a European Union of States of shared sovereignty. Each of these reforms would necessarily affect the others. Electoral reform—surely a necessary condition of healthy and accountable local and regional, national, and European government—would increase popular participation in the governing process of a much wider cross-section of the electorate and would promote a greater sense of community and of political pluralism. The creation of a Scottish Parliament and regional assemblies and executives would profoundly alter the composition and functions of the Westminster Parliament, and would influence the way in which the House of Lords was reformed. The enactment of a Bill of Rights,

© The Political Quarterly Publishing Co. Ltd. 1995.

even of the most modest kind based on the European Convention, would alter the nature of, the relationship between, and the functioning of the Judiciary, the Legislature and the Executive. Abridging the Executive's prerogative powers, and creating a right of access to official information, would transform the peoples of the United Kingdom from British subjects of the Crown into fully informed citizens with civil and political rights and duties derived from our citizenship.

Tony Blair, Gordon Brown, and Robin Cook, together with other Labour MPs like Giles Radice, Graham Allen, Tony Wright and Tessa Jowell, would support all or most of these reforms. So, too, would, for example, Derry Irvine, Raymond Plant and Tessa Blackstone in the Lords. But they are still only a small influential minority within the Parliamentary Labour Party. A Labour government will not be a midwife for constitutional change unless the reformers can win the hearts and minds of a broad cross-section of the Labour Party.

This will be difficult enough to achieve. But the most perplexing political conundrum is not *whether* this ambitious agenda of reforms is needed or has sufficient popular support, but *how* it can be achieved within a framework of coherent constitutional principles, with all deliberate speed, and in a manner which commands the confidence of the citizens on whose behalf the measures are to be enacted. The Labour Party is modernising its constitution under Tony Blair's bold leadership; but would a future government led by Tony Blair really modernise the British constitution? Obviously, it is essential that the Ministers responsible for constitutional reform should have the necessary political will, skill and clout.

Plainly, a first prerequisite is that, upon winning power, our political leaders should be and should remain committed to securing a constitutional settlement, and that Prime Minister Blair should make his dispositions accordingly. That is obvious, but it cannot be taken for granted even if Labour were to give unequivocal manifesto undertakings to the electorate.

Harold Wilson's second administration was elected in 1974 with a clear manifesto commitment to creating a more open process of government, in which the burden would be placed upon Whitehall to justify withholding official information from the public. Yet, as I too well recall as Special Adviser to Home Secretary Roy Jenkins, only three other members of the Wilson Cabinet took the commitment seriously enough to want to override senior civil servants' self-interested objections to Roy Jenkins' modest proposals for reform. When it came to the crunch, the manifesto promise was broken by the Wilson and Callaghan governments because of the absence of the necessary political will at senior ministerial level. All that the public were given instead was a woolly Green Paper.

I also too well recall how difficult it was to translate the manifesto commitment to sex and race discrimination legislation into practical reality. So obstructive were some Home Office officials with whom I

125

© The Political Quarterly Publishing Co. Ltd. 1995.

initially worked that I was sent home by Roy Jenkins to write what became the White Paper, 'Equality for Women', and later the Sex Discrimination Act 1975, and its counterpart, the Race Relations Act 1976.

When we produced a thoroughly balanced Green Paper on the incorporation of the European Human Rights Convention into UK law, there was a sustained attempt by senior civil servants to prevent it from being published, lest it should give the people dangerous ideas. By a bare majority, Ministers overcame official opposition, but the Home Office won in the end. The Green Paper was published not by HMSO but by the Home Office, and was read by almost no-one. The recommendations by the Standing Advisory Commission on Human Rights in Northern Ireland in 1977 that the European Convention should be made enforceable in our courts were similarly obstructed and ultimately buried.

It would be terribly easy for constitutional reform to suffer a similar fate next time, unless it is taken as seriously as the Thatcherites took their mission of breaking trade union and local government power and privatising public services. Our political leaders may *say* the right things about breaking the old constitutional mould, but would they be able to *do* the right things when faced with the crushing burdens of office, and with senior civil servants profoundly antagonistic to the reform programme? Would Labour Ministers be as bold and inventive in devising new legislative techniques as the Tories have been (witness the horrible but imaginative Deregulation and Contracting-out Act)? Or would the new government merely flirt with the idea of a new constitutional settlement without being willing or able to take sufficiently radical steps to achieve it?

A comprehensive approach to constitutional reform

What do I mean by sufficiently radical steps? To bring about a genuine new constitutional settlement, it would, in my view, be necessary to introduce a new way of law-making in place of the traditional British parliamentary diet of piecemeal, politically partisan and indigestible legislation. Unlike other Commonwealth and European countries which acquired their constitutions when they won their independence after revolutions or wars, we British cannot declare independence against ourselves. We have exported many written constitutions to the countries of the former British Empire, but we cannot easily import any of them into the 'mother country'. Yet somehow, if we are to achieve a system of government in which each part relates sensibly to the system as a whole, we must do the next best thing. We must work for a *comprehensive* programme of constitutional reforms rather than for yet another series of disjointed legislative acts.

We should try to convince our political leaders about this, as well as about the need to be and to remain firmly committed to the enterprise. We need to persuade them to resist the natural British political tendency of

© The Political Quarterly Publishing Co. Ltd. 1995.

opting for a series of separate pieces of controversial legislation—a Human Rights Bill, a Voting Reform Bill, a Scotland Bill, a Wales Bill, a Regional Government Bill, a Local Government Bill, a Hereditary Peers (Disqualification) Bill, a Freedom of Information Bill, a Machinery of Justice Bill, a Civil Service Bill, and so on. That is the natural tendency for future Ministers, because that has been the traditional way—deep-rooted in our political culture—in which governments of left and right have gone about translating their manifesto promises into reality: by means of specific legislation to deal with particular problems, incrementally and one piece at a time. That is what the Treasury, the Lord Chancellor's Department, the Home Office, the Cabinet Office, and the Law Officers' Department will argue is the only way forward.

It would be a great temptation for Tony Blair's Cabinet to adopt this traditional approach, because it seems so sensible and so politically expedient: sensible, because it is in the British tradition of pragmatism; politically expedient, because it enables the package of constitutional reforms to be unpacked and fitted more easily into an overcrowded legislative programme according to the political needs of a government beset by the problems of fashioning its economic, fiscal and social policies. But it is a deadly political trap.

A rational and orderly constitutional settlement would not be readily achieved by slicing its subject-matter into a series of separate Bills, each making incremental changes. That has been the 'pragmatic' way in which the Conservatives have legisled in the fields of employment, education, criminal justice and local government: by means of one Bill after another spread over the sixteen years in which they have so far controlled the legislative machine. The Thatcher and Major Governments have had plenty of time; they have been single-minded, and they have got their way. But I doubt whether even their best friends would commend it as a way of making rational and user-friendly laws.

In any event, it is certainly not a politically intelligent way of enacting measures which will fit together into a sensible constitutional framework of democratic and accountable government. In theory, it would be possible for a series of separate and free-standing Bills to be drafted within a framework of constitutional principles drawn up by Whitehall. But it is improbable that Parliament—unguided and unrestrained by such a frame- work—would enact the legislation in such a neatly logical and orderly way.

What is much more likely is that, for reasons of political expediency, there will be no attempt by a Labour government to create the framework of a new constitutional settlement, and that what will be achieved instead will be some useful but limited tinkering with the mess of statutes, conven- tions, customs, and judicial decisions which together constitute the British constitution and its laws.

I accept that there would be no need to agree upon a framework of constitutional principle before taking the important but modest and technically easy step of enacting a Human Rights Bill, along the lines of my

© The Political Quarterly Publishing Co. Ltd. 1995.

Private Member's Bill, to incorporate the European Convention into the domestic laws of the United Kingdom. The passage of such a Bill would be relatively smooth, because the public authorities of the UK are already bound by the Convention, and Parliament could not alter the terms of the Convention in the process of domesticating its provisions without being in breach of international law. It would therefore make good sense to introduce such a Bill at an early stage (as Labour apparently intends), without awaiting the much more complex process of legislating for the rest of the constitutional package. The same applies to a Freedom of Information Bill.

It would be much more hazardous to attempt to enact the rest of the reform programme in separate legislative bits and pieces, and without a set of overall guiding constitutional principles. There are many cautionary lessons from previous attempts of that kind undertaken by governments committed to reform, undone by badly designed half-measures. Let me give just two examples from the experience of Harold Wilson's and Jim Callaghan's administrations: Scottish and Welsh devolution, and House of Lords reform.

Devolution

The strenuous but clumsy and grudging efforts of two successive Labour governments between 1974 and 1979 to devolve legislative and executive powers to Scotland and Wales were flawed from the beginning, because what was introduced was not a well-conceived constitutional measure, but a highly swollen and obsessively detailed version of a Local Government Bill.

The congenitally defective Scotland and Wales Bill, introduced into Parliament in 1976, met heavy opposition and eventually had to be withdrawn in early 1977 when a cross-party alliance defeated a guillotine motion. The Bill was then divided into two. Both remaining Bills dominated the session and were passed only when an amendment was made requiring the two Assemblies to be approved by a referendum in which more than 40 per cent of eligible voters gave their support.

The definition of what was and of what was not to be devolved in these Bills was not based on constitutional principles or standards, but on lengthy and obsessively detailed lists of specific functions, designed to preserve Ministers' powers and a unitary State. The government and its advisers were deeply hostile to a genuinely federal scheme in which the elected Assemblies would have limited revenue-raising powers, and in which the independent courts (by means of judicial review) rather than Ministers (by means of the political exercise of their executive powers) would protect the scope and limits of the devolved powers. They did not understand what a workable federal system means, and what they did understand, they disliked. Very reluctantly, Ministers eventually had to concede a role for the Judicial Committee of the Privy Council in deciding

128

© The Political Quarterly Publishing Co. Ltd. 1995.

on the legislative competence of the Scottish Assembly, but they were unable to devise a scheme which was sufficiently popular among those in Scotland who seek home rule within the United Kingdom.

If the Scotland Act 1978 and the Wales Act 1978 had come into operation, they would have enacted the most important change in our constitution since the replacement of the English and Scottish Parliaments by the Parliament of Great Britain in 1707, and the ending of the coerced union with Ireland in 1922. The Acts did not come into operation, because they failed to obtain the necessary 40 per cent support of the total electorate in the referenda held in Scotland and Wales in 1979. The threshold was weighted in favour of the status quo, and failed narrowly in Scotland and by a margin of four to one in Wales.

The devolution story is an object lesson in how not to engage in constitutional reform, yet it is a lesson which may not have been learnt. A future Labour government seems all too likely to succumb to the temptation to try to rush a Scottish Parliament Bill through in its first year in office. It will not want to wait to devise and enact a federal system of regional government; nor will it want to weaken its political base at Westminster by reducing the number of Scottish MPs as a consequence of creating a Scottish Parliament.

On this basis, the difficult questions raised by Labour opponents of the Scotland and Wales Bill in the 1970s, led by the brilliant duo of Tam Dalyell and George Cunningham, will remain unanswered. There is the so-called West Lothian question, raised so insistently and effectively by Tam Dalyell: how can it be right that he, as MP for West Lothian, would no longer be entitled to vote at Westminster on matters transferred to the Scottish Parliament, while still being able to vote on English affairs? And there are the other hard questions too. How many MPs should Scotland continue to have at Westminster after much of Scotland's political business has shifted north of the Border? Should there be a Secretary of State for Scotland, and, if so, with what remaining functions?

These questions can only be answered satisfactorily within a proper federal framework. We must try to persuade Tony Blair and his colleagues that it would be politically wise and expedient to legislate for Scottish Home Rule, not in isolation, but as part of a sensible constitutional scheme.

The House of Lords

To take another example: Tony Blair announced at the Labour Party's Blackpool conference that his Government would bring in a measure in its first year to reform the House of Lords by abolishing the voting rights of hereditary peers. Of the hereditary peers (including peers of first creation) 336 are Conservative, 25 are Liberal Democrat, only 12 are Labour, and 174 are Cross-Bench. So Labour would lose only 10 per cent of its peers, while Liberal Democrats would lost almost half of theirs.

© The Political Quarterly Publishing Co. Ltd. 1995.

I agree that hereditary peers would have to lose their voting rights as part of the reform process. But if that were all that was done, it would leave an undemocratic quango of nominated peers, still with a substantial built-in Conservative majority. To produce a Labour majority in the Lords, the Blair government would have to use its political patronage on a large scale so as to pack the Labour benches with its placemen and placewomen. To rectify the under-representation of Liberal Democrats, the Blair government would also have to be generous about increasing our representation. (I should declare an interest as a Liberal Democrat placeman!)

The exercise of so much political patronage would not look very attractive for a government committed to replacing quangos with democratically accountable institutions. It would not enhance the democratic credentials or constitutional legitimacy of the Upper House, nor would it give the Lords a distinctive parliamentary function, different from that of the Commons, notably in relation to the regions. No doubt it is regarded merely as a temporary political expedient, and it might be necessary to adopt it on that basis. But the political imperative ought surely to be to reform the Lords as part of a cogent and convincing constitutional scheme, which is clear about the distinctive role and functions of the Upper House, for example, as a constitutional watchdog with power to veto Commons legislation in conflict with constitutional principles, and/or as a UK forum with duty to represent and protect the interest of the regions and nations, along the lines of the German Bundesrat.

I wonder whether Mr Blair's constitutional advisers have studied the fate of the first Wilson Government's bungled attempt to reform the House of Lords in accordance with Labour's manifesto commitment? The story is expertly and sensitively told in Dr Janet Morgan's fascinating study, *The House of Lords and the Labour Government 1964–1970*, OUP, Oxford, 1975.

The problem was not in the Lords, which behaved with political intelligence and sensitivity and gave the White Paper's proposals their approval by 251 votes to 56, with only a minority disapproving in each Party. It was the Commons which stifled the Parliament (No. 2) Bill. It was given a Second Reading, but the real battle occurred at Committee Stage. Since 1945, by convention, Bills on major constitutional matters are not sent to a Standing Committee, but are committed to a Committee of the Whole House; and when they are taken on the Floor of the House there are great possibilities for filibusters and other obstructive ploys.

The Wilson Government originally allowed only five days for the Committee Stage on the Floor of the House. After twelve days and over eighty hours in Committee, only the preamble and five clauses had been debated. A skilful all-party Back Bench alliance, from Michael Foot on the left to Enoch Powell on the right, exploited every Commons procedural device to obstruct the Bill's passage. Some wanted to leave the Lords as it was, either because they approved of it, or because they hoped it would wither away. Others wanted outright abolition; some had alternative

130

© The Political Quarterly Publishing Co. Ltd. 1995.

schemes of reform. Eventually, in what had now become a debacle, the government was forced to abandon the Bill altogether. Labour's Election Manifesto in May 1970 promised further proposals, but House of Lords' reform had become a subject which future governments would need to handle with great care.

Perhaps a short and crudely simple Bill, of the kind now contemplated by Labour to abolish the voting rights of hereditary Peers, would speedily be enacted next time. The danger is that, even if this happened, the government would damage its constitutional credibility in the process, and jeopardise the reform programme as a whole. At the very least, the Lords' reform debacle of the 1960s, like the devolution shambles of the 1970s, shows how difficult it will be to enact constitutional measures which have to be taken on the Floor of the House of Commons.

A constitutional convention

Is there any other method of constitutional law-making which would respect Parliament's sovereign legislative powers and yet avoid these pitfalls? Is there a way to ease the passage of the legislation in a manner which would make constitutional sense and be likely to survive a future change of government? I believe that there are several ways which respect both parliamentary sovereignty and popular sovereignty.

For example, the opposition parties might set out in their election manifestos not only the basic principles of the constitutional programme of reform which they seek to implement, but also the means by which they will seek to do so. They could undertake to enact legislation at an early stage, establishing a Constitutional Convention to draw up the terms of the new settlement. The Convention would be chaired by a senior Law Lord and would consist of well-qualified men and women from across the United Kingdom, within and beyond Parliament, from all political parties and from none. Unlike another sadly wasted opportunity born of a Labour government—the Kilbrandon Royal Commission on the Constitution 1969–1973—a well-constructed and well-directed Constitutional Convention would be an effective means of promoting public education about the need for a new settlement, of preparing a well-rounded scheme, of circumventing Whitehall resistance, and of limiting parliamentary opposition.

A Constitutional Convention appointed and working on this basis, with a strong team of advisers, would enjoy unique authority and influence. Provided that it was well-supported within the government, it would have a sufficient critical mass to become the engine of reform. The un-elected Convention would still need to win democratic legitimacy for its proposals—unlike the many ill-considered and partisan measures which Mrs Thatcher's and Mr Major's Governments have originated, centralising public powers at the expense of local elected governments, and contracting out the public service to unaccountable private bodies.

131

© The Political Quarterly Publishing Co. Ltd. 1995.

The manifestos could therefore promise that the enabling legislation would provide that, before it came into force, the terms of the new settlement (or some of them) would be submitted to the peoples of the United Kingdom for their approval, whether by election or referendum.

In theory the Conservative Party and their supporters could refuse to participate in such a process of reform, but I doubt whether they would boycott it, provided that the Constitutional Convention were sufficiently broad-based and authoritative to command widespread popular support, and provided also that its proposals would be put to the nation as a whole. Parliament could obstruct the process, just as the Lords blocked Gladstone's second Irish Home Rule Bill a century ago. But I doubt whether they would do so when it came to the political crunch, in the light of the mandate given by the voters to the incoming government.

The main disadvantage of creating a Constitutional Convention is that it would enable a faint-hearted government to kick the controversial and complex subject into touch for several years, only to face formidable difficulties later about persuading Parliament to enact the Convention's scheme. Another way of tackling the problem would be for the new government to publish a draft Bill, in the first session of a reform-minded Parliament, encompassing the various interrelated proposals for constitutional reform, and to submit the Bill to a large cross-party Select Committee of the House of Commons (and, perhaps, concurrently to a similar Committee of the House of Lords, or even to a Joint Select Committee of both Houses). The Committee or Committees would take evidence and report back to Parliament, recommending which major issues of principle should be debated on the floor of the Commons and which should be entrusted to a Standing Committee for detailed consideration. This would comply with the Labour Party's undertaking to proceed with legislation in the first session of Parliament, and would avoid the possible difficulty of putting tough questions requiring political resolution into commission. It might also ease the subsequent passage of the legislation.

Of course I do not argue dogmatically that these are the only means of achieving sensible constitutional reform. There are no doubt other possibilities which should be considered. Those of us who see a pressing need for a new constitutional deal might remember Judge Learned Hand's warning that 'the spirit of liberty is the spirit that is not too sure that it is right'.

Nor do I advocate a formal Lab-Lib. Dem. election pact, because I believe that a formal pact would diminish the prospects of ousting the present Government. But if both opposition parties committed themselves, in parallel, openly and before the next election, to such a constitutional reform programme and to the means they intend for achieving it, they would increase their chances of being trusted with powers by a majority of their fellow citizens, and of being able to use that power to secure a sensible and lasting settlement based upon constitutional principles.

132

© The Political Quarterly Publishing Co. Ltd. 1995.

© The Political Quarterly Publishing Co. Ltd. 1995. Published by Blackwell Publishers, 108 Cowley Road, Oxford OX4 1JF, UK and 238 Main Street, Cambridge, MA 02142, USA.

INDEX

134

© The Political Quarterly Publishing Co. Ltd. 1995.

INDEX

investment 40
  in the environment 47–8, 53–4

Japan 58
Jenkins, Roy 127
justice 42–3

Keynes, J. M. 54
Keynesianism 9, 21

Labour Force Survey 1994 65
Labour movement 97, 98
Labour Party/Governments 12–13,
  123, 124–5, 126–7, 129–32
law, European 115, 116–18
Left 23
  economic agenda for 54
  global approach of 56–60
  and local development policy 83–7
Lele, S. 33
Liberal Democratic Party 123, 131
liberalism 24–5, 84
  see also neo-liberalism
life expectancy 95
Liverpool 100
living standards, differences in 93, 97
local councillors 102–3
local development policy 14, 79–81
  Left and 83–7
  models for 81–2
local government 13, 49, 88, 101–3,
  125
lone parents 90, 107, 112

Maastricht Treaty 113, 115–16, 117,
  118, 119, 120
Machin, S. 106
macroeconomic management 45
Major, John 118, 119
Manchester 101
manufactured capital 38
marginalisation 22, 106–7
market economy 6, 13, 85
marriage 108
Marshall, T. H. 113, 116
means-tested benefits 111
Mexico, local development in 82
migrant workers 59
Mill, J. S. 5
monetary policy 58

monetary union 12
morality 89–92
Morgan, Janet 131
multinational capital 31
Murray, Charles 108

nation state 13, 14, 80
national accounts 50
national sovereignty 12–13, 114
nationalisation 12
nationalist movements 20
neighbourhood councils 101
neo-liberalism 11–12, 13, 84, 85
Netherlands, and the European
  Community 117, 118
network organisations 80, 83, 85–6
New Right 2, 13
  individualism 5–8
New York Times 20
Nicoll, William 117
non-standard jobs 62, 67

opportunity 24–5, 26, 27
Orbach, Susie 109
Organisation for Economic Co-
  operation and Development
  Employment Outlook 69
output 74

Paine, Thomas 5
parents, responsibilities of 109
Parliament Bill 131–2
part-time employment 70–1
Pearce, D. 33
planning 9
  environment and 47
pluralism 14
political citizenship 116–20, 123
Polluter Pays Principle 43, 47
pollution 50
poverty 37, 43, 93–4, 106–7
power 13–14, 84, 85
  balance of 10
privatism 25, 26
privatism 25, 26
privatisation 25, 26
production 37–8, 39, 84
  internationalisation of 80
productivity 55
progressive politics 84–7
public ownership 6, 7

135

© The Political Quarterly Publishing Co. Ltd. 1995.

136

© The Political Quarterly Publishing Co. Ltd. 1995.

© The Political Quarterly Publishing Co. Ltd. 1995.